Contents

Key to map pages

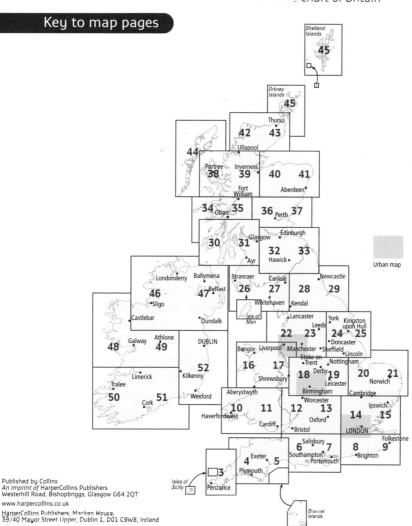

Published by Collins
An imprint of HarperCollins Publishers
Westerhill Road, Bishopbriggs, Glasgow G64 2QT
www.harpercollins.co.uk

HarperCollins Publishers, Macken House,
39/40 Mayor Street Upper, Dublin 1, D01 C9W8, Ireland

Copyright © HarperCollins Publishers Ltd 2023

Collins® is a registered trademark of HarperCollins Publishers Limited

Contains Ordnance Survey data © Crown copyright and database right (2022)

Mapping generated from CollinsBartholomew digital databases

The grid on this map is the National Grid taken from the Ordnance Survey map with
the permission of the Controller of Her Majesty's Stationery Office.

© Natural England copyright. Contains Ordnance Survey data © Crown copyright
and database right (2022)

The contents of this publication are believed correct at the time of printing.
Nevertheless, the publisher can accept no responsibility for errors or omissions,
changes in the detail given, or for any expense or loss thereby caused.

The representation of a road, track or footpath is no evidence of a right of way.

Printed in China

ISBN 978 0 00 859761 0

10 9 8 7 6 5 4 3 2 1

e-mail: roadcheck@harpercollins.co.uk

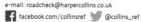
facebook.com/collins_ref   @collins_ref

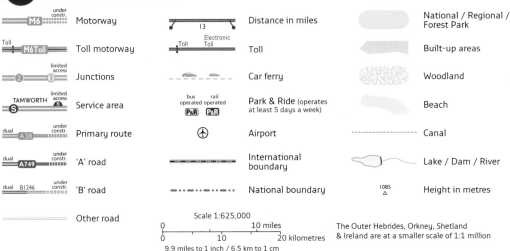

Motorway
Toll motorway
Junctions
Service area
Primary route
'A' road
'B' road
Other road

Distance in miles
Toll
Car ferry
Park & Ride (operates at least 5 days a week)
Airport
International boundary
National boundary

National / Regional / Forest Park
Built-up areas
Woodland
Beach
Canal
Lake / Dam / River
Height in metres

Scale 1:625,000
0   10 miles
0   10   20 kilometres
9.9 miles to 1 inch / 6.5 km to 1 cm

The Outer Hebrides, Orkney, Shetland & Ireland are at a smaller scale of 1:1 million

Urban area map symbols

1:285,714   4.5 miles to 1 inch / 2.9 km to 1 cm

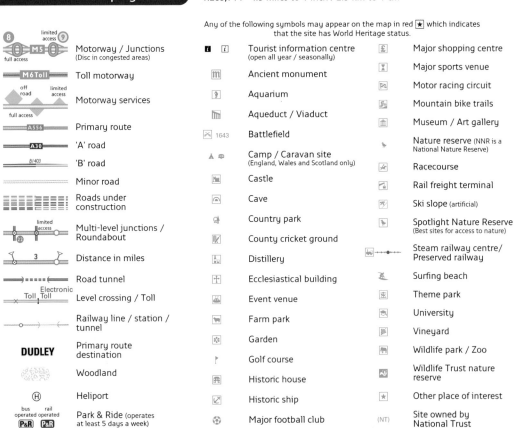

Any of the following symbols may appear on the map in red ★ which indicates that the site has World Heritage status.

Motorway / Junctions (Disc in congested areas)
Toll motorway
Motorway services
Primary route
'A' road
'B' road
Minor road
Roads under construction
Multi-level junctions / Roundabout
Distance in miles
Road tunnel
Level crossing / Toll
Railway line / station / tunnel
Primary route destination
DUDLEY
Woodland
Heliport
Park & Ride (operates at least 5 days a week)

Tourist information centre (open all year / seasonally)
Ancient monument
Aquarium
Aqueduct / Viaduct
Battlefield
Camp / Caravan site (England, Wales and Scotland only)
Castle
Cave
Country park
County cricket ground
Distillery
Ecclesiastical building
Event venue
Farm park
Garden
Golf course
Historic house
Historic ship
Major football club

Major shopping centre
Major sports venue
Motor racing circuit
Mountain bike trails
Museum / Art gallery
Nature reserve (NNR is a National Nature Reserve)
Racecourse
Rail freight terminal
Ski slope (artificial)
Spotlight Nature Reserve (Best sites for access to nature)
Steam railway centre/ Preserved railway
Surfing beach
Theme park
University
Vineyard
Wildlife park / Zoo
Wildlife Trust nature reserve
Other place of interest
Site owned by National Trust (NT)

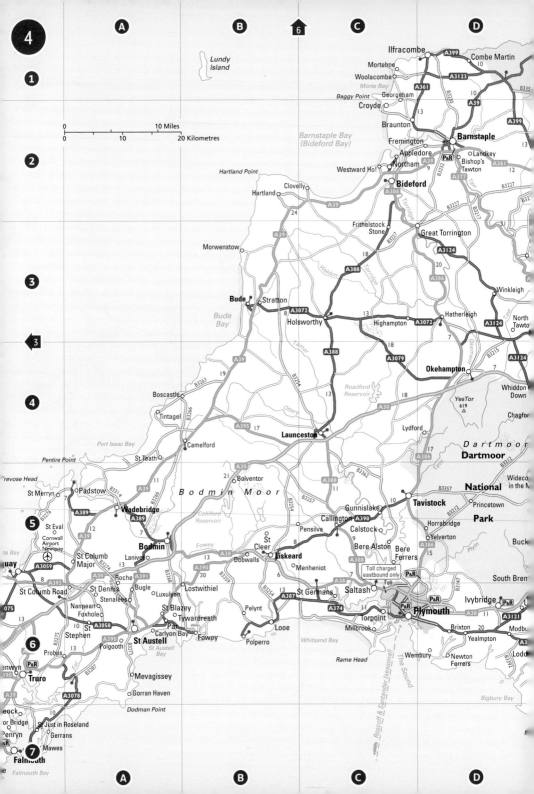

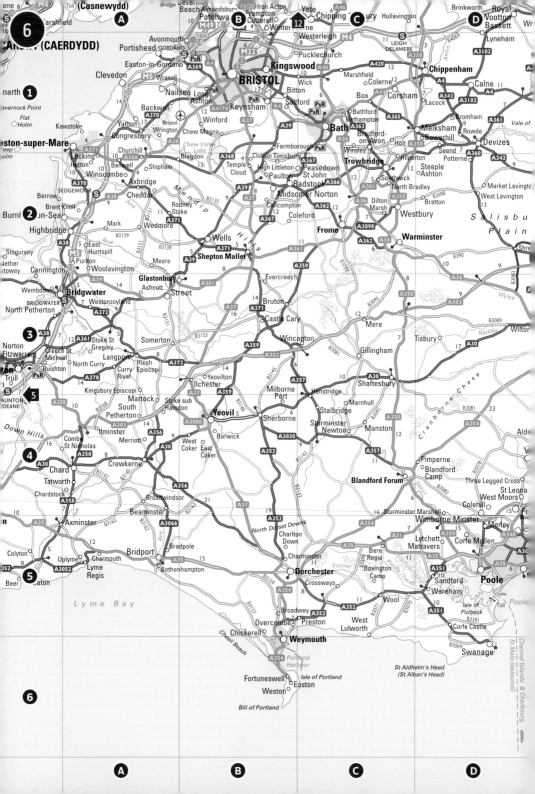

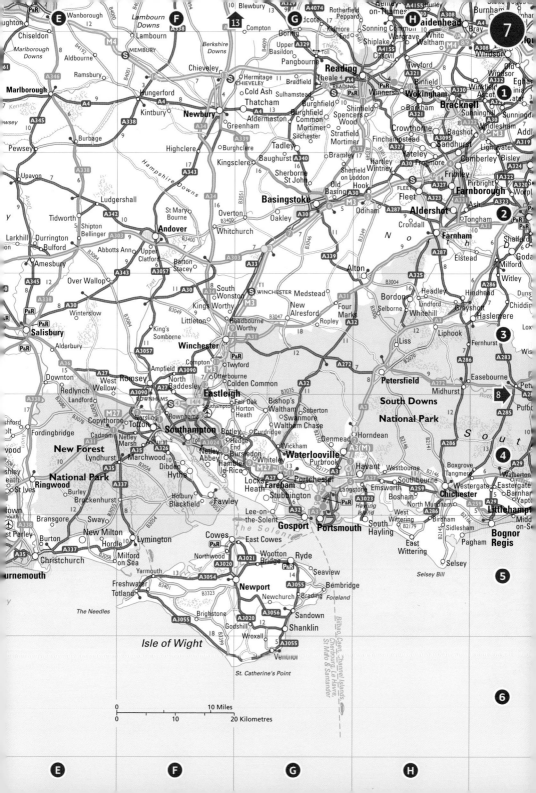

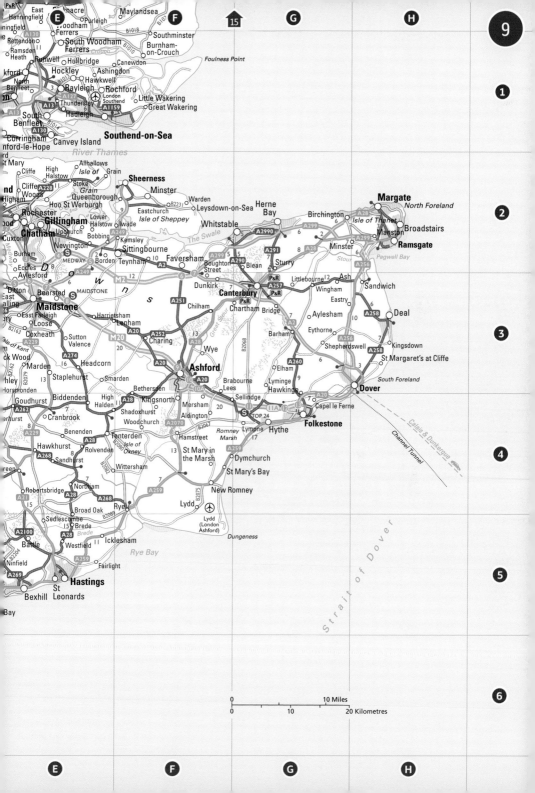

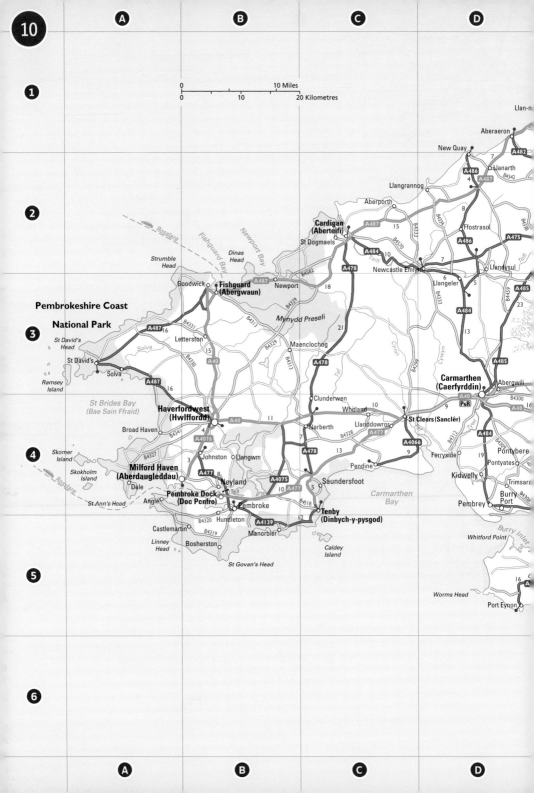

10

A   B   C   D

1

0   10 Miles
0   10   20 Kilometres

Llan-n

Aberaeron

New Quay   A482

2   7
A486   Llanarth
4   A487   B4342

Llangrannog

Aberporth   8   Ffostrasol   A486   A475

Rosslare

Fishguard Bay

Newport Bay   Cardigan (Aberteifi)   A487   15   B4333

St Dogmaels

Dinas Head   B4570   B4334

A484   10   *Teifi*   7   Llandysul

A478   Newcastle Emlyn   A485

Strumble Head   6   B4459

Goodwick   A487   Newport   18   Llangeler   5

Fishguard (Abergwaun)   B4582

B4333   A484   23

Pembrokeshire Coast   *Mynydd Preseli*   21

National Park   A487   16   B4313   B4329

St David's Head   Letterston   15   Maenclochog   13

3   *Solva*   B4330   B4313   A478   A485

St David's   A40   *Cynin*   **Carmarthen (Caerfyrddin)**

St David's   Solva   A487   16   *Taf*   B4299   Abergwili

Ramsey Island   B4300

Clunderwen   10   A40   A48

St Brides Bay (Bae Sain Ffraid)   **Haverfordwest (Hwlffordd)**   A40   11   Whitland   9   **St Clears (Sanclêr)**   A484

Broad Haven   B4341   Narberth   B4328   Llanddowror   A477   A4066   B4312

4   A4076   4   7   A478   13   Ferryside   19   Pontyberem

Skomer Island   3   Johnston   Llangwm   Pendine   9   Pontyates   Trimsara

Skokholm Island   **Milford Haven (Aberdaugleddau)**   A477   Neyland   A4075   Saundersfoot   Kidwelly   **Burry Port**

Rosslare   Dale   10   A477   5   *Carmarthen Bay*   Pembrey

St Ann's Head   Angle   **Pembroke Dock (Doc Penfro)**   B4318

            Pembroke   12   **Tenby (Dinbych-y-pysgod)**   *Whitford Point*   *Burry Inlet*

Castlemartin   B4320   Hundleton   A4139   Manorbier

Linney Head   B4319   Bosherston   *Caldey Island*

5   *St Govan's Head*   *Worms Head*   16   A

                                                 Port Eynon

6

A   B   C   D

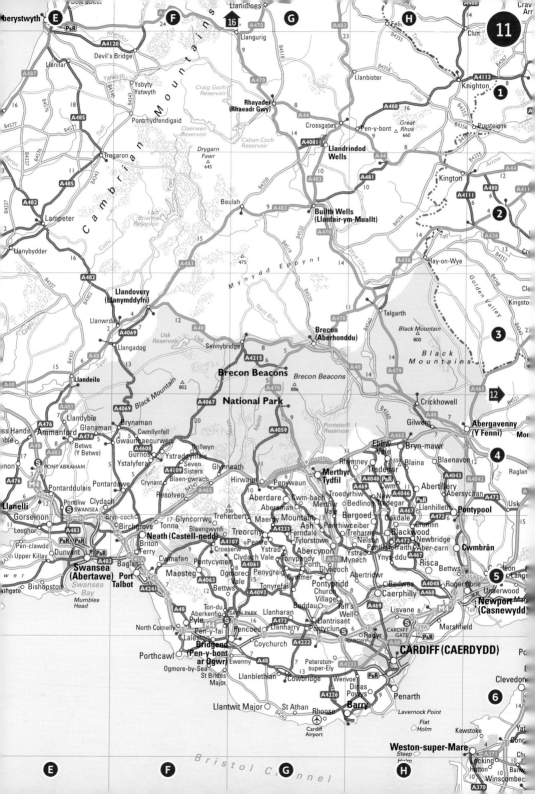

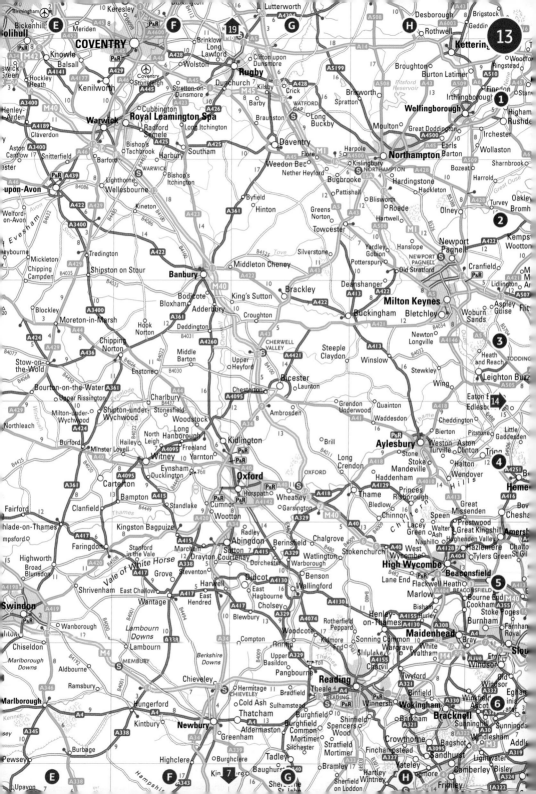

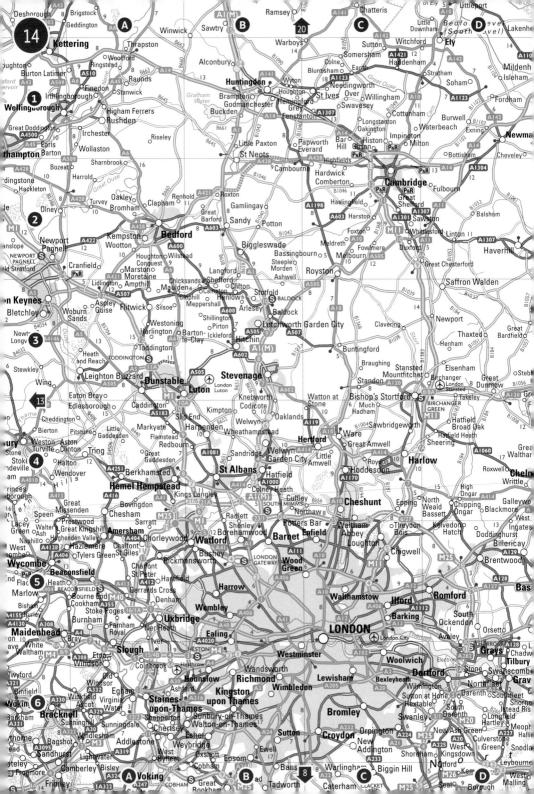

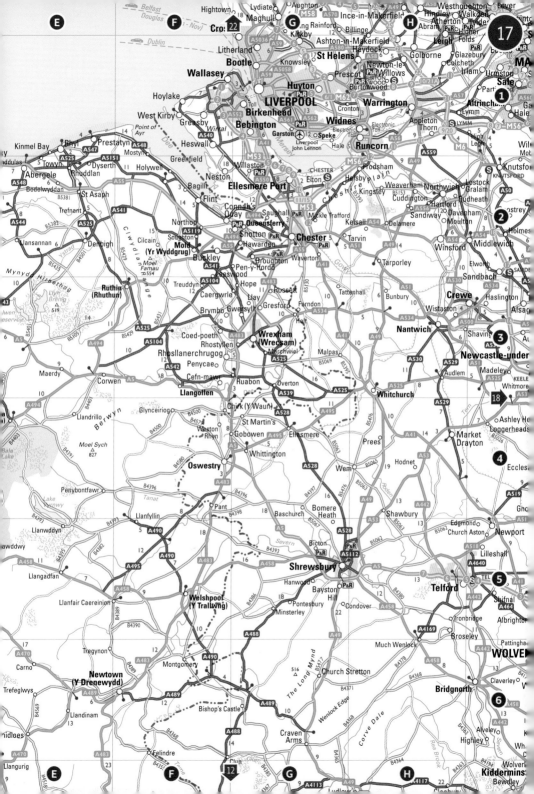

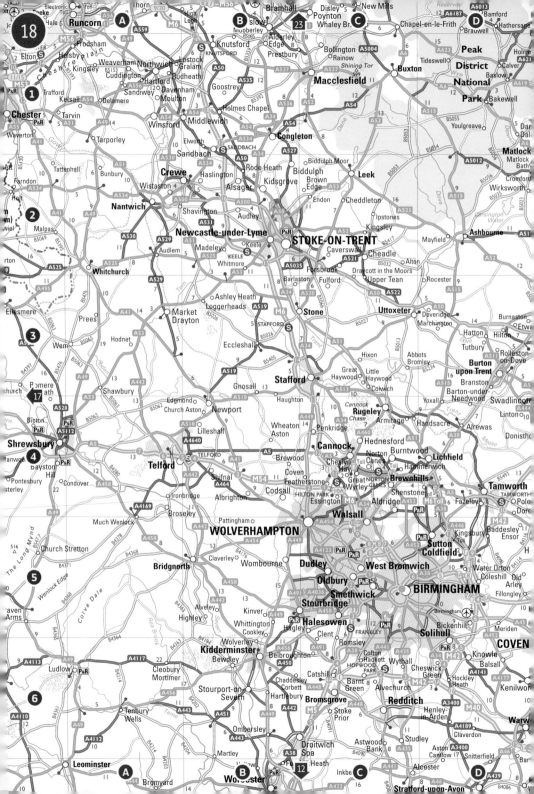

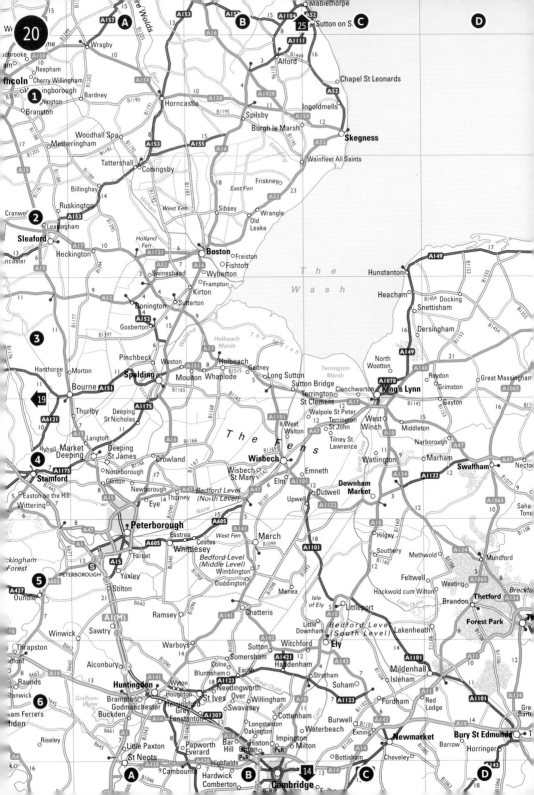

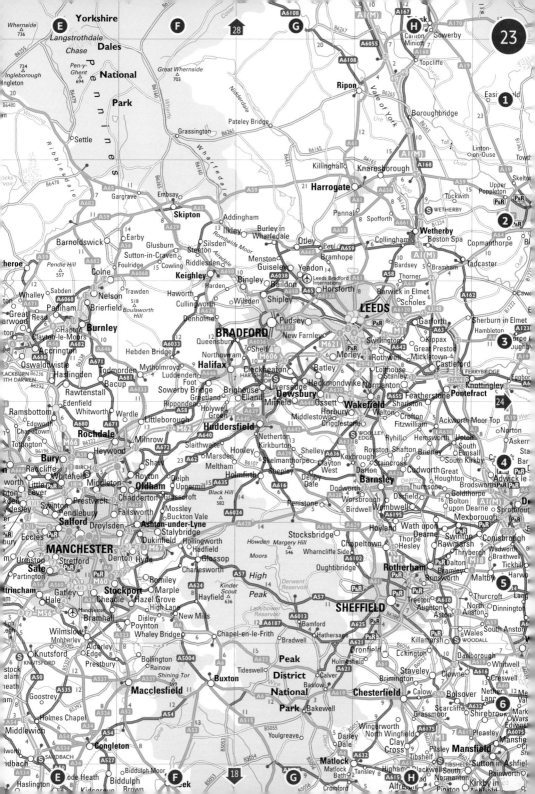

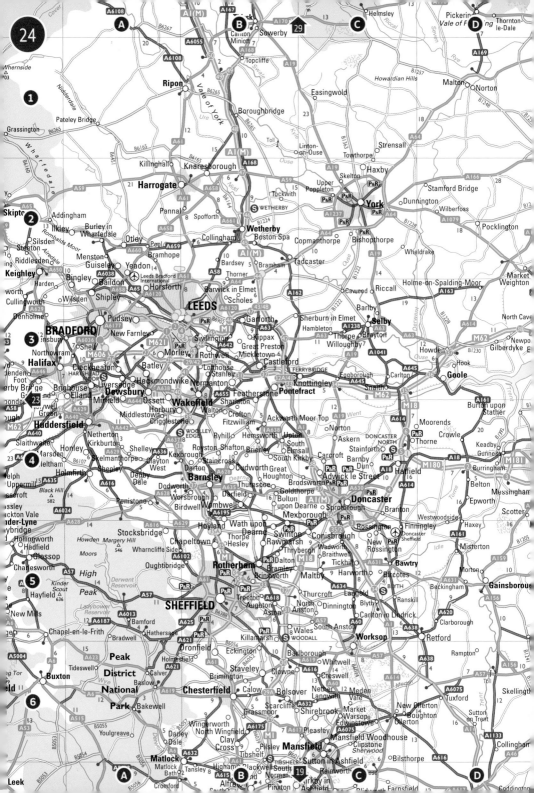

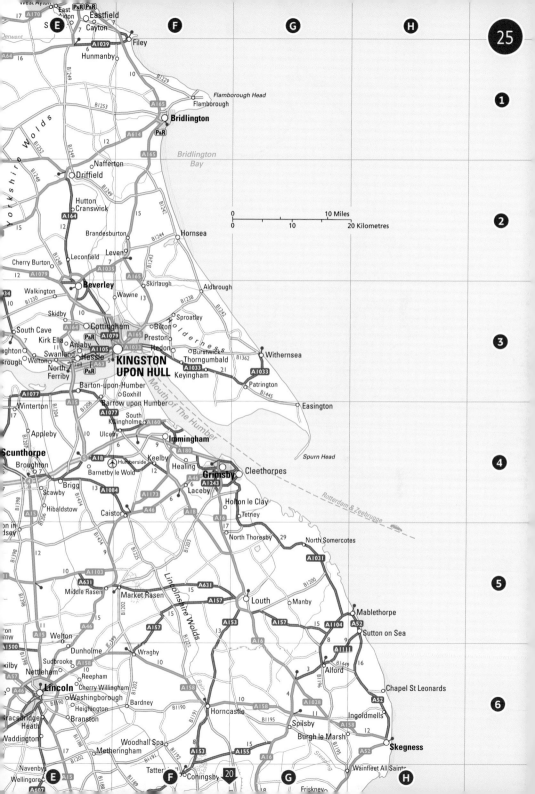

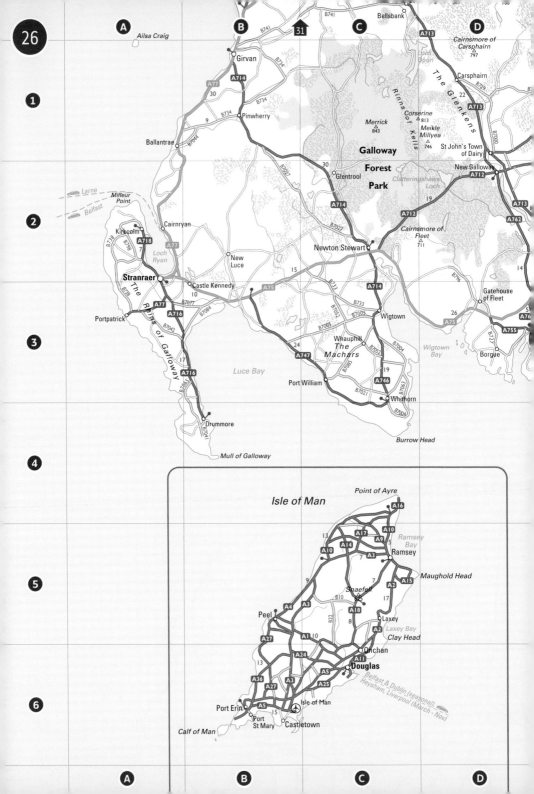

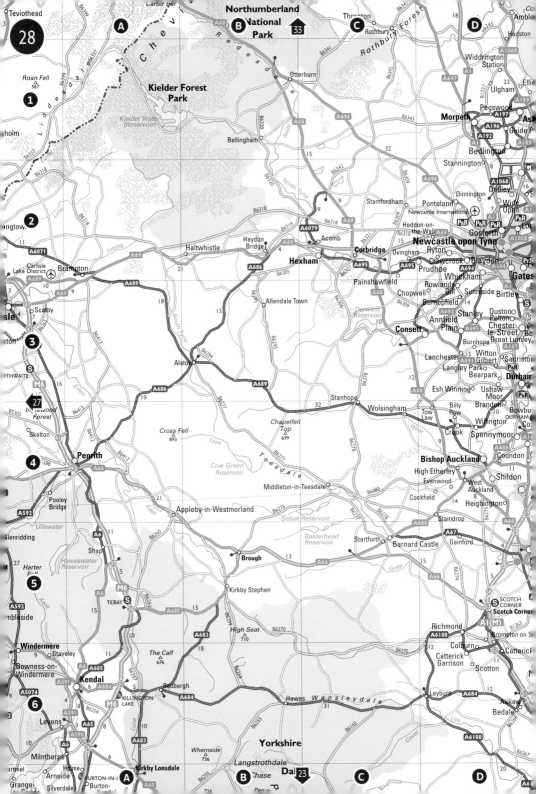

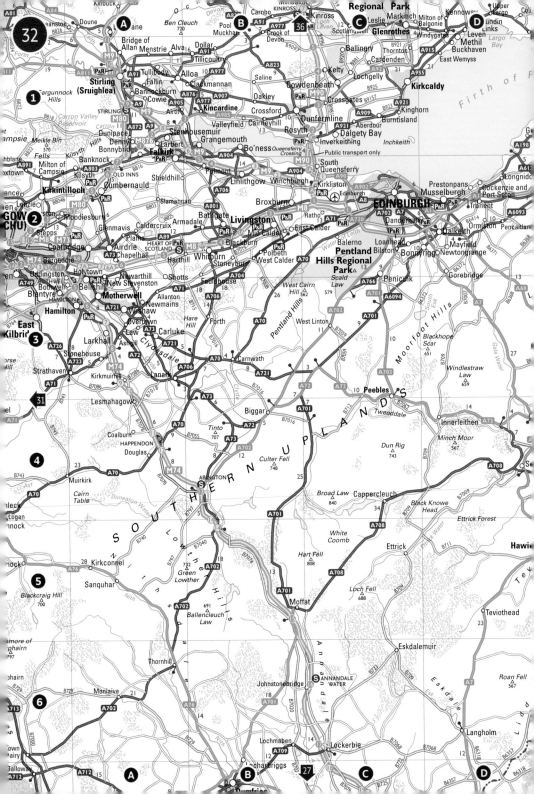

E **F** **G** **H**

Kilrenny
Anster
Pittenweem
St Monans
Kilconquhar
St Monans

Isle of May

Bass Rock
North Berwick
East Linton
Dunbar
Haddington

1

2

Meikle Black Law
St Abb's Head
Eyemouth
A1107
A6112
B6438
B6437
Chirnside
Foulden
Berwick-upon-Tweed
Lammer Law 528
Meikle Says Law 535
Whiteadder Water
Dirrington Great Law
Duns
A6105
Paxton
B6460
Scremerston
Westruther
A697
B6456
A6105
B6460
A6089
A6105
Gordon
B6364
B6461
A697
Coldstream
A698
A6112
B6355
Holy Island
Burrows Hole
Farne Islands
B6353
Cockenheugh 211
Bamburgh
Seahouses
North Sunderland
Beadnell Bay
Cornhill on Tweed
Crookham
B6353
B6352
B6354
Belford
B6349
B6348
Leader Water
Earlston
Smailholm
Gordon
Kelso
A699
St Boswells
Newtown St Boswells
A699
A68
Melrose
A6089
A698
B6396
B6352
B6397
B6404
B6398
B6356
B6361
B6352
B6352
Town Yetholm
Wooler
Cateran Hill
A697
B6346
B6347
B1340
B1342
Longhoughton
A1
Jedburgh
Ancrum
Denholm
A698
B6400
B6358
B6357
A68
The Cheviot 815
Windy Gyle 619
Powburn
Alnwick
Bonchester Bridge
A6088
B6399
Carter Bar
A68
Northumberland National Park
Whittingham
Thropton
Rothbury
B6341
Shilbottle
Warkworth
Coquet Island
Amble
Hadston
A1068
B6345
5

3

Tweed
Blackadder Water
12
15
13
3
9
13
15
8
10
11
10
13
8
12
12
12
14
5
7
9
13
12
14
18
12

Kielder Forest Park
Kielder Water (Reservoir)
A68
Cheviot Hills
Redesdale
Otterburn
B6320
B6341
B6342
Widdrington Station
A1068
A1
Ellington
Lynemouth
Ulgham
23
Pegswood
Newbiggin-by-the-
Morpeth
A197
A196
A1068
6

Bellingham
North Tyne
28
B6342
B6343
A68
A696
A696
B6309
32
15
Stannington
Ashington
Guide Post
A192
Bedlington
A189
Blyth
Cramlington
Seaton Sluice
A1068
Seaton Delaval

E **F** **G** **H**

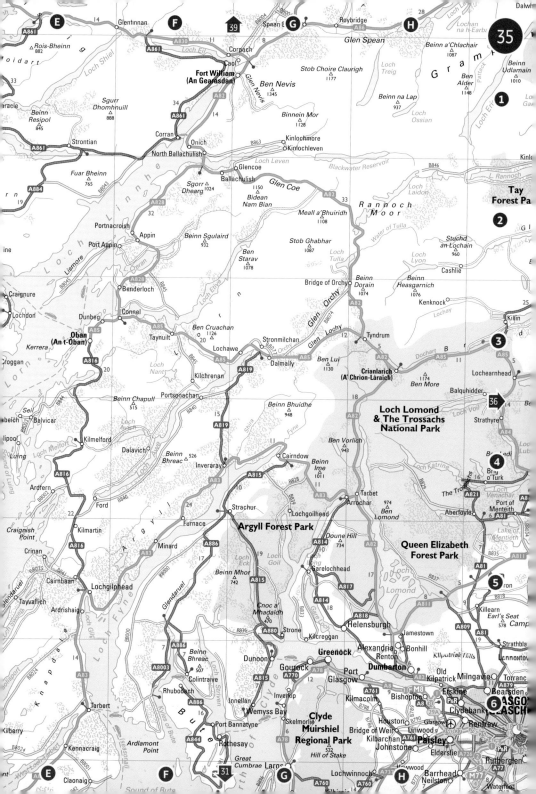

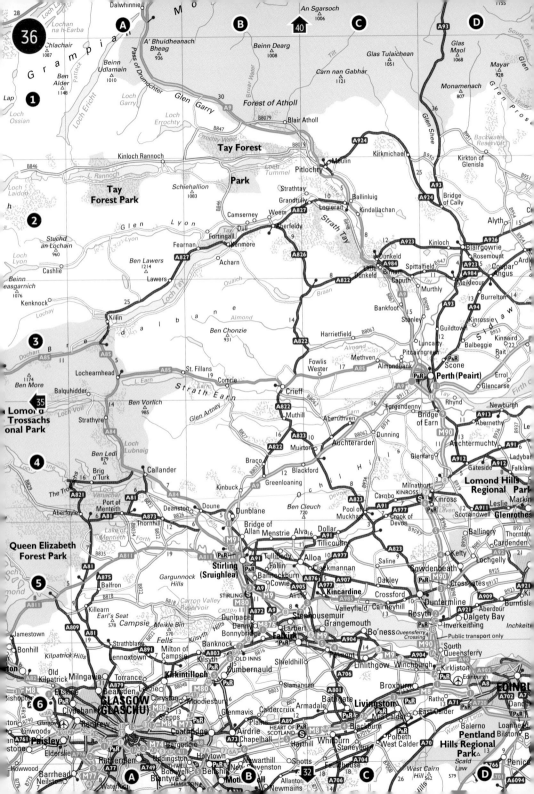

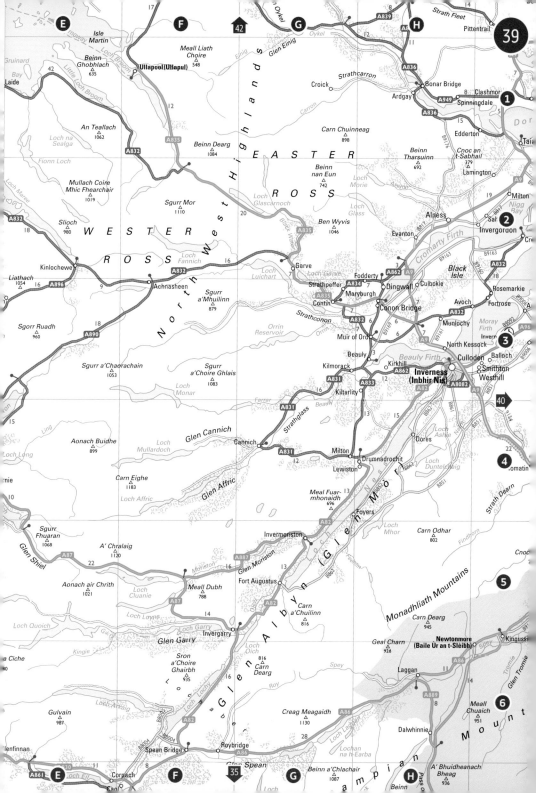

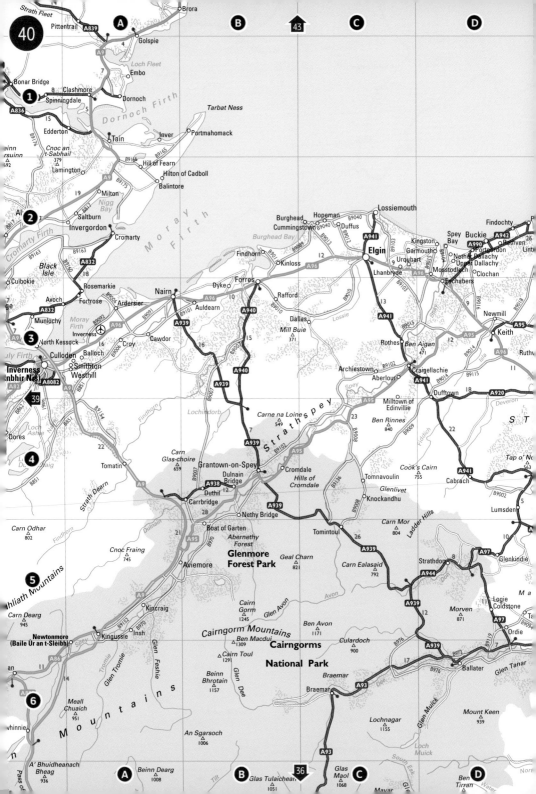

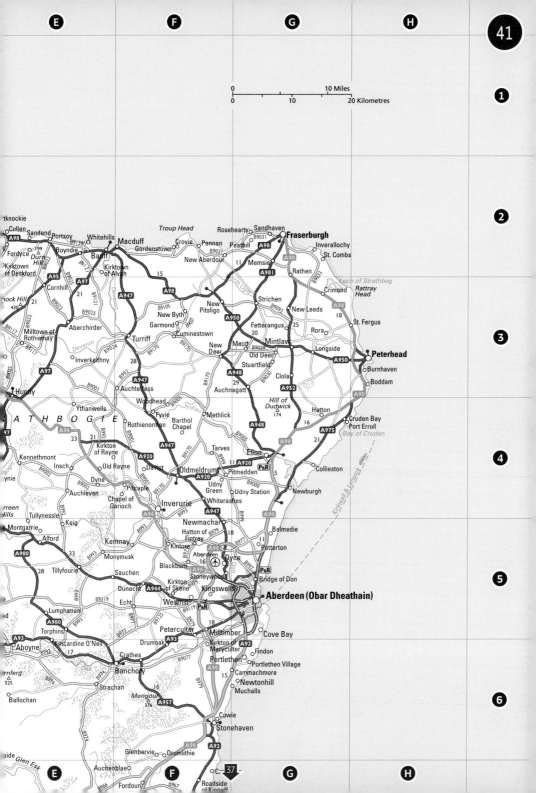

E   F   G   H

1

2

10 Miles
0   10   20 Kilometres

Fraserburgh
Rosehearty Sandhaven
Troup Head   B9031
tknockie   Inverallochy
Cullen Sandend Portsoy Whitehills   Crovie Pennan Peathill A98 St. Combs
A98   Gardenstown   Memsie A90
Fordyce 199 Boyndie Macduff   New Aberdour 11   Rathen B9033
Durn Kirktown   Banff   Loch of Strathbeg
Kirktown Hill of Alvah   A981   Crimond Rattray
of Deskford A95 B9025 Kirktown   Strichen B9091   Head
Cornhill A97 B9121 of Alvah A98   New B9105   New Leeds A90
nock Hill 21   15   Pitsligo   18 St. Fergus
430   B9025   New Byth   Garmond Fetterangus   Rora
B9117 Milltown of   Aberchirder B9024 Cuminestown 20 Mintlaw 25
Rothiemay B9117 Deveron   Turriff B9170 Maud B9029 Longside **Peterhead**
Huntly A97 B992 Inverkeithny 28 B9001 New A948 Old Deer A950 Burnhaven
THBOGIE B9001   Auchterless Deer B9170 Stuartfield Boddam
97   A96 Ythanwells Woodhead B9005 Auchnagatt 29 Clola A952
Kennethmont 23 21 Rothienorman Barthol Methlick Hill of Hatton
B992 Kirkton Fyvie Chapel   Dudwick 16 Cruden Bay
Insch A920 of Rayne A947 B9170 Tarves B9005 174 A975 Port Erroll
nie Old Rayne Daviot   Elion A90 21 Bay of Cruden
Auchleven Oyne Pitcaple Oldmeldrum 111 A920 Collieston
Chapel of B9002 B9170 A920 Udny B9000
rreen Garioch Inverurie Pitmedden Green Newburgh
ills Keig A96 A947 Whiterashes Udny Station
Montgarrie Alford B993 Newmachar Balmedie
A980 Kemnay Hatton of B977 11 Potterton
33 Monymusk Fintray 18 A90
Tillyfourie Sauchen Kintore A90
28   Kirkton Blackburn Aberdeen Dyce
Lumphanan Dunecht A944 of Skene Stoneywood Bridge of Don
Torphins B9119 Echt Kingswells **Aberdeen (Obar Dheathain)**
A93 Aboyne B993 Westhill
Kincardine O'Neil 17 Peterculter 18 Cove Bay
Drumoak A93 Milltimber Findon
Crathes Kirkton of A92 Portlethen
Banchory Maryculter Cammachmore Portlethen Village
rnferd 525 B9077 Portlethen 15 Newtonhill
Strachan 16 B979 Muchalls
Mongour 376 A957 Cowie
Ballochan B974   Stonehaven
A90
ide Glen Esk Glenbervie Drumlithie A92
Auchenblae 37 Roadside
Fordoun B967 of Kinneff

E   F   G   H

3

4

5

6

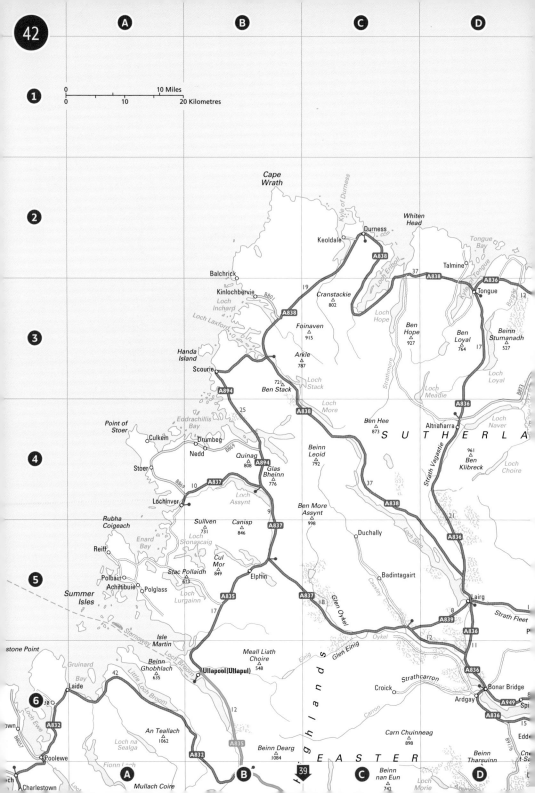

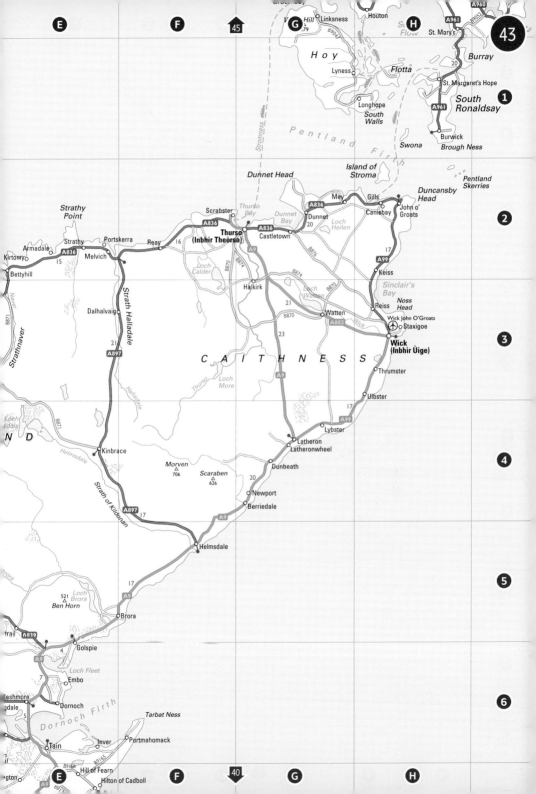

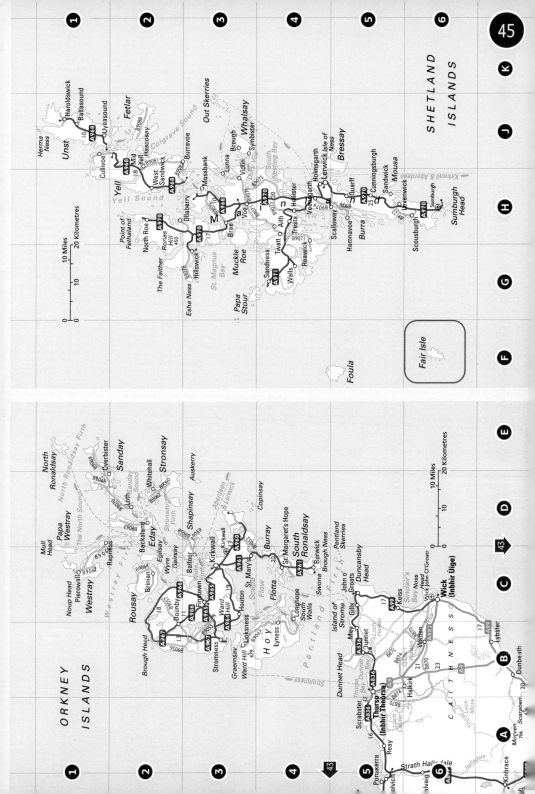

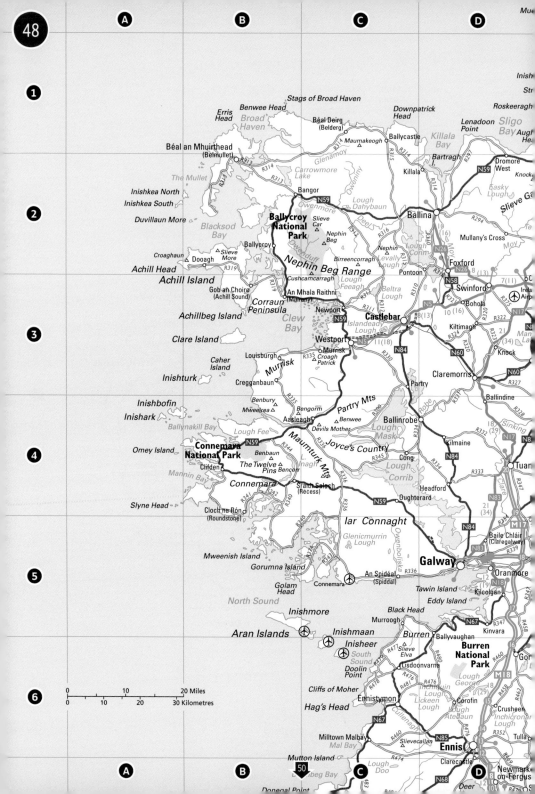

A B C D

Mu

1

Inish
Str
Roskeeragh

2

Stags of Broad Haven
Benwee Head
Erris Head
Downpatrick Head
Béal Deirg (Belderg)
Broad Haven
Béal an Mhuirthead (Belmullet)
Maumakeogh
Ballycastle
Lenadoon Point
Killala Bay
Sligo Bay
Augh He.
Glenamoy
Bartragh I.
The Mullet
Carrowmore Lake
Killala
Dromore West
Knock.
Inishkea North
Inishkea South
Bangor
Owenny
Lough Dahybaun
Ballina
Easky Lough
Slieve Ga
Duvillaun More
Owenmore
Ballycroy National Park
Slieve Car
Nephin Beg
Lough Conn
Mullany's Cross
Moy
Blacksod Bay
Ballycroy
Nephin
Foxford
Croaghaun
Slieve More
Nephin Beg Range
Birreencorragh
Pontoon
Swinford
Irela Airp
Man
La
Dooagh
Achill Head
Achill Island
Cushcamcarragh
Lough Feeagh
Beltra Lough
N58
Gob an Choire (Achill Sound)
An Mhala Raithní (Mulrany)
Lough Levally Lough
Kiltimagh
Bohola
Corraun Peninsula
Newport
Castlebar
Achillbeg Island
Clew Bay
Islandeady Lough
Knock
Clare Island
Westport
Murrisk
Croagh Patrick
Partry
Claremorris
Caher Island
Louisburgh
Ballindine
Inishturk
Cregganaun
Murrisk
Robe
Partry Mts
Ballinrobe
Kilmaine
Inishbofin
Benbury
Bengorm
Benwee
Lough Mask
Kilmaine
Inishark
Mweelrea
Aasleagh
Devils Mother
Joyce's Country
Ballynakill Bay
Lough Fee
Maumturk Mts
Omey Island
Connemara National Park
Benbaun
The Twelve Pins
Bencorr
Cong
Lough Corrib
Tuan
Clifden
Connemara
Sraith Salach (Recess)
Headford
Mannin Bay
Iar Connaght
Oughterard
Slyne Head
Cloch na Rón (Roundstone)
N59
Mweenish Island
Glenicmurrin Lough
Owenboliska
Baile Chláir (Claregalway)
Gorumna Island
Galway
Golam Head
An Spidéal (Spiddal)
Connemara
Oranmore
North Sound
Tawin Island
Kilcolgan
Eddy Island
Inishmore
Murroogh
Black Head
Aran Islands
Inishmaan
Burren
Ballyvaughan
Kinvara
Inisheer
South Sound
Slieve Elva
Burren National Park
Gor
Doolin Point
Lisdoonvarna
Cliffs of Moher
Lough George
Inchiquin Lough Lickeen
Inchicronan Lough
Ennistymon
Corofin
Crusheen
Hag's Head
Lough Atedaun
Tulla
Milltown Malbay
Mal Bay
Slievecallan
Ennis
Mutton Island
Lough Doo
Clarecastle
Newmark on-Fergus
Donegal Point
Bay
Deer

N59 N26 N5 N17 N84 N60 N17 N8 M17 N18 N67 M8 N67 N85 N68

3

4

5

6

0 10 20 Miles
0 10 20 30 Kilometres

50

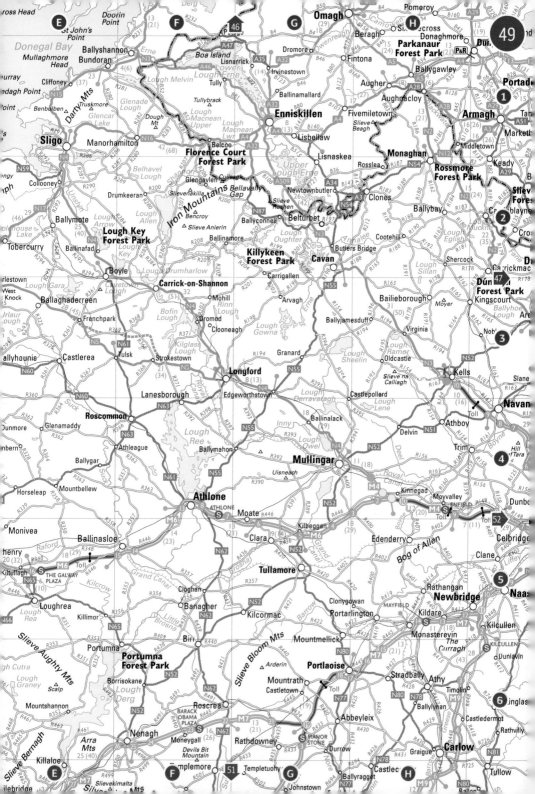

In general, distances are based on the shortest routes by classified roads.
Where a route includes a ferry journey, the distance is circled.

DISTANCE IN KILOMETRES

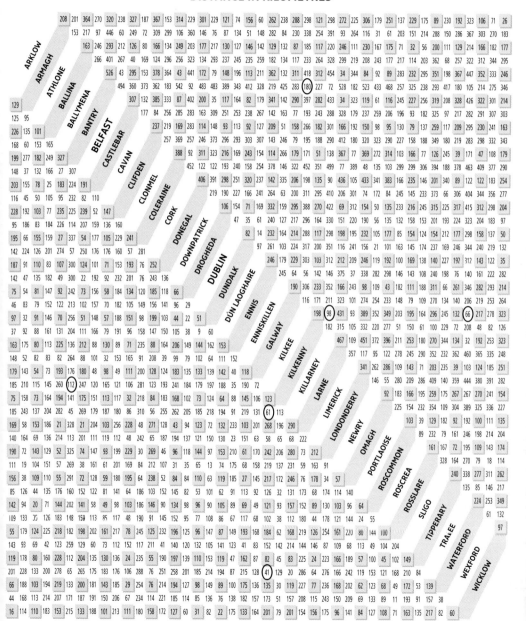

DISTANCE IN MILES

Abbreviations

Aber.	Aberdeenshire	E.Suss.	East Sussex	N.N'hants.	North Northamptonshire	Staffs.	Staffordshire
Arg. & B.	Argyll & Bute	Flints.	Flintshire			Stir.	Stirling
B'burn.	Blackburn with Darwen	Glos.	Gloucestershire	N.Som.	North Somerset	Suff.	Suffolk
Bed.	Bedford	Gt.Lon.	Greater London	N.Yorks.	North Yorkshire	Surr.	Surrey
Brack.F.	Bracknell Forest	Gt.Man.	Greater Manchester	Norf.	Norfolk	Swin.	Swindon
Bucks.	Buckinghamshire	Hants.	Hampshire	Northumb.	Northumberland	T. & W.	Tyne & Wear
Cambs.	Cambridgeshire	Here.	Herefordshire	Notts.	Nottinghamshire	Tel. & W.	Telford & Wrekin
Caerp.	Caerphilly	Herts.	Hertfordshire	Ork.	Orkney	V. of Glam.	Vale of Glamorgan
Cen.Beds.	Central Bedfordshire	High.	Highland	Oxon.	Oxfordshire	W'ham	Wokingham
Chan.I.	Channel Islands	I.o.M.	Isle of Man	P. & K.	Perth & Kinross	W.Berks.	West Berkshire
Ches.E.	Cheshire East	I.o.W.	Isle of Wight	Pembs.	Pembrokeshire	W.Loth.	West Lothian
Ches.W. & C.	Cheshire West & Chester	Lancs.	Lancashire	Peter.	Peterborough	W.Mid.	West Midlands
		Leics.	Leicestershire	R. & C.	Redcar & Cleveland	W.N'hants.	West Northamptonshire
Cornw.	Cornwall	Lincs.	Lincolnshire	R.C.T.	Rhondda Cynon Taff		
Cumb.	Cumbria	M.K.	Milton Keynes	S.Ayr.	South Ayrshire	W.Suss.	West Sussex
D. & G.	Dumfries & Galloway	Med.	Medway	S.Glos.	South Gloucestershire	W.Yorks.	West Yorkshire
Darl.	Darlington	Mersey.	Merseyside	S.Lan.	South Lanarkshire	Warks.	Warwickshire
Denb.	Denbighshire	Midloth.	Midlothian	S.Yorks.	South Yorkshire	Warr.	Warrington
Derbys.	Derbyshire	Mon.	Monmouthshire	Sc.Bord.	Scottish Borders	Wilts.	Wiltshire
Dur.	Durham	Na H-E. Siar	Na H-Eileanan Siar	Shet.	Shetland	Worcs.	Worcestershire
E.Ayr.	East Ayrshire		(Western Isles)	Shrop.	Shropshire	Wrex.	Wrexham
E.Loth.	East Lothian	N.Lan.	North Lanarkshire	Slo.	Slough		
E.Riding	East Riding of Yorkshire	N.Lincs.	North Lincolnshire	Som.	Somerset		

Note: Bold entries refer to Urban maps pages 54-59

A

Abberley 56 A6
Abberley Common 56 A6
Abbey Wood 55 F4
Abbots Bromley 18 C3
Abbots Langley 54 B1
Abbotsfield Farm 58 D3
Abbotskerswell 5 E5
Aberaeron 10 D1
Aberaman 11 G4
Aber-carn 11 H5
Aberchirder 41 E3
Abercynon 11 G5
Aberdare 11 G4
Aberdaron 16 A4
Aberdeen (Obar Dheathain) 41 G5
Aberdour 32 C1
Aberdovey Aberdyfi 16 C6
Aberfeldy 36 D2
Aberfoyle 31 H1
Abergavenny (Y Fenni) 12 A4
Abergele 22 A6
Abergwili 10 D3
Abergynolwyn 16 C5
Aberkenfig 11 F5
Aberlemno 37 F2
Aberlour (Charlestown of Aberlour) 40 C3
Abernethy 36 D4
Aberporth 10 C2
Abersoch 16 B4
Abersychan 11 H4
Abertillery 11 H4
Abertridwr 11 H5
Aberuthven 36 C4
Aberystwyth 16 C6
Abingdon 13 F5
Aboyne 41 E6
Abram 22 D4
Abram 59 E2
Abridge 55 F2
Accrington 23 E3
Acharacle 34 D1
Acharn 36 B2
Achiltibuie (Achd-'Ille-Bhuidhe) 42 A5
Achmore 44 E3
Achnasheen 39 F3
Ackleton 56 A3
Ackworth Moor Top 24 B4
Acle 21 G4
Acock's Green 57 E4
Acomb 28 C2

Acton Gt.Lon. 54 C3
Acton Suff. 15 E2
Acton Worcs. 56 B6
Acton Bridge 58 D5
Acton Trussell 56 C1
Adderbury 13 F3
Addingham 23 F2
Addington Gt.Lon. 55 E5
Addington Kent 55 H6
Addiscombe 55 E5
Addlestone 14 A6
Addlestone 54 B5
Adeney 56 A1
Adeyfield 54 B1
Adlington Ches.E. 59 H4
Adlington Lancs. 22 D4
Adlington Lancs. 58 D2
Adwick le Street 24 C4
Affetside 59 F1
Aigburth 58 B4
Aimes Green 55 F1
Ainsdale 58 B1
Ainsdale-on-Sea 58 B1
Ainsworth 59 F1
Aintree 58 B3
Aird of Sleat 38 C5
Airdrie 32 A2
Airidh a' Bhruaich 44 D4
Airth 32 A1
Aiskew 28 D6
Aith 45 H4
Albrighton 18 B4
Albrighton 56 B2
Alcester 12 D2
Alconbury 14 B1
Aldbourne 13 E6
Aldbrough 25 F3
Aldeburgh 15 H2
Aldenham 54 C2
Alderbury 7 E3
Alderholt 7 E4
Alderley Edge 23 E6
Alderley Edge 59 G5
Aldermaston 13 G6
Aldershot 7 H2
Aldingham 9 F4
Aldridge 18 C4
Aldridge 56 D2
Alexandria 31 G3
Alfold 8 A4
Alford Aber. 41 E5
Alford Lincs. 25 G6
Alfreton 19 E2
Allanton 32 A3
Allendale Town 28 B3
Allerton 58 C4
Allesley 57 F4
Allgreave 59 H6

Allhallows 15 E6
Allimore Green 56 B1
Allithwaite 22 C1
Alloa 32 A1
Allostock 59 F5
Allscot 56 A3
Almondbank 36 C3
Almondsbury 12 B3
Alness 39 H2
Alnwick 33 H5
Alperton 54 C3
Alresford 15 F3
Alrewas 18 D4
Alrewas 57 E1
Alsager 18 B2
Alston 28 B3
Alstone 56 B1
Alt 59 H2
Altnaharra 42 D4
Alton Hants. 7 H3
Alton Staffs. 18 C2
Altrincham 23 E5
Altrincham 59 F4
Alva 32 A1
Alvanley 58 C5
Alvechurch 12 D1
Alvechurch 56 D5
Alvecote 57 F2
Alveley 18 B5
Alveley 56 A4
Alveston 12 B5
Alyth 36 D2
Amble 33 H5
Ambleside 56 B4
Ambleside 27 H5
Ambrosden 13 G4
Amersham 14 A5
Amersham 54 A2
Amesbury 7 E2
Amington 57 F2
Amlwch 16 B1
Ammanford (Rhydaman) 11 E4
Ampfield 7 F3
Ampthill 14 A3
Ancaster 19 H2
Ancrum 33 E4
Anderton 59 E5
Andover 7 F2
Anfield 58 B3
Angle 10 A4
Angmering 8 A5
Anlaby 25 E3
Annan 27 G2
Annfield Plain 28 B3
Ansley 18 D5
Ansley 57 F3
Anstey 19 F4

Anstruther 37 F4
Ansty 57 G4
Antrobus 59 E5
Apeton 56 B1
Appin (An Apainn) 35 F2
Appleby 25 E4
Appleby Magna 19 E4
Appleby Magna 57 G1
Appleby Parva 57 G2
Appleby-in-Westmorland 28 A4
Applecross 38 D3
Appledore 4 C2
Appleton 56 D4
Appleton Thorn 22 D5
Appleton Thorn 59 E4
Appley Bridge 22 D4
Appley Bridge 58 D2
Apsley 54 B1
Arbirlot 37 F2
Arbroath 37 F2
Archiestown 40 C3
Arclid 59 F6
Ardbeg 30 B4
Ardersier 40 A3
Ardfern 30 D1
Ardgay 39 H1
Ardingly 8 C4
Ardleigh 15 F3
Ardleigh Green 55 G3
Ardler 36 D2
Ardminish 30 C4
Ardrishaig 30 D2
Ardrossan 31 F4
Ardvasar 38 C5
Ardwick 59 G3
Areley Kings 56 B5
Arinagour 34 B2
Arisaig (Àrasaig) 38 C6
Arkley 54 D2
Arlesey 14 B3
Arley 59 E4
Armadale High. 43 E2
Armadale W.Loth. 32 B2
Armitage 18 C4
Armitage 56 D1
Arnisdale (Arnasdal) 38 D5
Arnold 19 F2
Arnside 22 C1
Arrochar 31 G1
Arundel 8 A5
Ascot 14 A6
Ascot 54 A5
Asfordby 19 G4
Ash Kent 9 G3
Ash Surr. 7 H2
Ash (New Ash Green) 55 H5

Ash Green 57 G4
Ashbourne 18 D2
Ashburton 5 E5
Ashby de la Zouch 19 E4
Ashby de la Zouch 57 G1
Aschurch 12 D3
Ashcott 6 A3
Ashford Hants. 7 E4
Ashford Kent 9 F3
Ashford Surr. 14 A6
Ashford Surr. 54 B4
Ashgill 32 A3
Ashill 20 D4
Ashingdon 15 E5
Ashington Northumb. 28 D1
Ashington W.Suss. 8 B5
Ashley 59 F4
Ashley Green 54 A1
Ashley Heath Dorset 7 E4
Ashley Heath Staffs. 18 B3
Ashow 57 G5
Ashtead 8 B4
Ashtead 54 C6
Ashton 58 D6
Ashton Keynes 12 D5
Ashton upon Mersey 59 F3
Ashton-in-Makerfield 22 D5
Ashton-in-Makerfield 58 D3
Ashton-under-Lyne 23 F5
Ashton-under-Lyne 59 H3
Ashurst 7 F4
Ashwell 14 B3
Askam in Furness 22 B1
Askern 24 C4
Aslockton 19 G2
Aspatria 27 G3
Aspley Guise 14 A3
Aspull 22 D4
Aspull 59 E2
Astbury 59 G6
Astle 59 G5
Astley Gt.Man. 59 F2
Astley Warks. 57 G4
Astley Worcs. 56 A6
Astley Abbotts 56 A3
Astley Bridge 59 F1
Astley Cross 56 B6
Astley Green 59 F3
Aston Ches.W. & C. 58 D5
Aston S.Yorks. 24 B5
Aston Shrop. 56 B3
Aston W.Mid. 56 D4
Aston Cantlow 12 E2
Aston Clinton 13 H4

Aston Fields 56 C6
Aston Flamville 57 H3
Aston Heath 58 D5
Aston-on-Trent 19 E3
Astwood Bank 12 D1
Astwood Bank 56 D6
Atherstone 19 E5
Atherstone 57 G3
Atherton 22 D4
Atherton 59 E2
Atterton 57 G3
Attleborough Norf. 21 E5
Attleborough
Warks. 57 G3
Auchenblae 37 G1
Auchencairn 27 E3
Auchinleck 31 H5
Auchleven 41 E4
Auchmithie 37 F2
Auchnagatt 41 G3
Auchterarder 36 C4
Auchterless 17 F3
Auchtermuchty 36 D4
Audenshaw 59 H3
Audlem 18 A2
Audley 18 B2
Aughton Lancs. 22 C4
Aughton Lancs. 58 B2
Aughton S.Yorks. 24 B5
Aughton Park 58 C2
Auldearn 40 B3
Aultbea
(An t-Allt Beithe) 38 D1
Austrey 57 F2
Aveley 14 D6
Aveley 55 G3
Avening 12 C5
Avery Hill 55 F4
Aviemore 40 A5
Avoch 40 A3
Avonmouth 12 B6
Awsworth 19 E2
Axbridge 6 A2
Axminster 5 G4
Aylesbury 13 H4
Aylesford 9 E3
Aylesham 9 G3
Aylsham 21 F3
Ayr 31 G5

B

Backaland 45 D2
Backford 58 C5
Backwell 12 A6
Bacup 23 E3
Baddesley Clinton 57 E5
Baddesley Ensor 18 D5
Baddesley Ensor 57 F3
Badger 56 A3
Badgerbank 59 G5
Badgers Mount 55 F5
Badsey 12 D2
Bagillt 22 B6
Bagillt 58 A5
Baginton 57 G5
Baglan 11 F5
Bagshot 14 A6
Bagshot 54 A5
Bagworth 57 H2
Baildon 24 A3
Bail' Ùr Tholastaidh 44 F2
Baile Ailein 44 D3
Baile Mòr 34 B3
Baker Street 55 H3
Bakewell 24 A6
Bala (Y Bala) 17 E4
Balbeggie 36 D3
Balchrick 42 B3
Balcombe 8 D4
Balderstone 59 H1
Balderton 58 B6
Baldock 14 B3
Balemartine 34 A2
Balerno 32 C2
Balfour 45 C3
Balfron 31 H2
Balham 54 D4
Balintore 40 A2

Balivanich (Baile a'
Mhanaich) 44 B7
Balla 44 B9
Ballachulish (Baile a'
Chaolais) 35 F2
Ballantrae 26 A1
Ballater 40 D6
Ballinger Common 54 A1
Ballingry 32 C1
Ballinluig 36 C2
Balloch 40 A3
Balls Hill 56 C3
Balmedie 41 G5
Balmerino 37 E3
Balmullo 37 E3
Balquhidder 36 A3
Balsall 13 E1
Balsall 57 F5
Balsall Common 57 F5
Balsall Heath 56 D4
Balsham 14 D2
Baltasound 45 J1
Balvicar 30 D1
Bamber Bridge 22 D3
Bamburgh 33 H4
Bamford 24 A5
Bamford 59 G1
Bampton Devon 5 F2
Bampton Oxon. 13 F4
Banbury 13 F2
Banchory 41 F6
Banff 16 C2
Bangor 16 C2
Bangor's Green 58 B2
Banham 21 E5
Bank Top 58 D2
Bankfoot 36 C3
Banknock 32 A2
Banks 22 C3
Bannockburn 32 A1
Banstead 8 B3
Banstead 54 D6
Banwell 6 A2
Bar Hill 14 C1
Barber's Moor 58 C1
Barby 13 G1
Bardney 25 F6
Bardon 57 H1
Bardsey 24 B2
Barford 13 E1
Barford 57 F6
Bargeddie 32 A2
Bargoed 11 H5
Barham 9 G3
Barkham 13 H6
Barking 14 C5
Barking 55 F3
Barking Riverside 55 F3
Barlaston 18 B3
Barlborough 24 B6
Barlby 24 C3
Barlestone 19 E4
Barlestone 57 H2
Barnacle 57 G4
Barnard Castle 28 C5
Barnby Dun 24 C4
Barnehurst 55 G4
Barnes 14 B5
Barnet 14 B5
Barnet Gate 54 D2
Barnetby le Wold 25 E4
Barnham 8 A5
Barnoldswick 23 E2
Barnsley 24 B4
Barnstaple 4 D2
Barnston 58 A4
Barnt Green 12 D1
Barnt Green 56 D5
Barnton 59 E5
Barrhead 31 H4
Barrow 15 E1
Barrow Nook 58 C2
Barrow upon Humber 25 E3
Barrow upon Soar 19 F4
Barrow-in-Furness 22 B1
Barrowby 19 G3
Barry 11 H6
Barston 57 F5

Barthol Chapel 41 F4
Bartley Green 56 D4
Barton 22 D3
Barton (Ormskirk) 58 B2
Barton Green 57 E1
Barton Stacey 7 F2
Barton in the Beans 57 G2
Barton-le-Clay 14 A3
Barton-under-Needwood
18 D4
Barton-under-Needwood
57 E1
Barton-upon-Humber 25 E3
Barvas (Barabhas) 44 E2
Barwell 19 E5
Barwell 57 H3
Barwick 6 B4
Barwick in Elmet 24 B3
Baschurch 17 G4
Bascote 57 H6
Basildon 15 E5
Basingstoke 7 G2
Baslow 24 A6
Bassingbourn 14 C2
Batchley 56 D6
Batchworth 54 B2
Batchworth Heath 54 B2
Bate Heath 59 E5
Bath 12 C6
Bathampton 12 C6
Bathford 12 C6
Bathgate 32 B2
Batley 24 A3
Battersea 54 D4
Battle 9 E5
Baughurst 7 G2
Bawtry 24 C5
Baxterley 57 F3
Bayford 55 E1
Bayston Hill 17 G5
Bayswater 54 D3
Beaconsfield 14 A5
Beaconsfield 54 A2
Beaminster 6 A4
Bean 55 G4
Bearley 57 E6
Bearpark 28 D4
Bearsden 31 H3
Bearsted 9 E3
Bearwood 56 D4
Beaudesert 57 E6
Beauly
(A' Mhanachainn) 39 H3
Beaumaris
(Biwmares) 16 C2
Beausale 57 F5
Bebington 22 C5
Bebington 58 B4
Beccles 21 G5
Beckbury 56 A2
Beckenham 55 E5
Beckingham 24 D5
Beckton 55 F3
Becontree 55 F3
Bedale 28 D6
Beddau 11 G5
Beddgelert 16 C3
Beddington 54 D5
Beddington Corner 54 D5
Bedford 14 A2
Bedlington 28 D1
Bedlinog 11 G4
Bedmond 54 B1
Bednall 56 C1
Bedol 58 A5
Bedworth 19 E4
Bedworth 57 G4
Bedworth
Woodlands 57 G4
Beechwood 58 D4
Beer 5 G4
Beeston 19 F3
Beeston Regis 21 F2
Beetley 21 E4
Beffcote 56 B1
Beith 31 G4
Belbroughton 12 D1
Belbroughton 56 C5
Belfield 59 H1

Belford 33 H4
Bell Bar 54 D1
Bell End 56 C5
Bell Heath 56 C5
Bellfields 54 A6
Bellingdon 54 A1
Bellingham Gt.Lon. 55 E4
Bellingham
Northumb. 28 B1
Bellsbank 31 G6
Bellshill 32 A3
Belmont 59 E1
Belmont (Harrow) 54 C2
Belmont (Sutton) 54 D5
Belper 19 E2
Belsize 54 B1
Belton N.Lincs. 24 D4
Belton Norf. 21 G5
Belvedere 55 F4
Bembridge 7 G5
Benderloch
(Meadarloch) 35 F3
Benenden 9 E4
Benllech 16 C1
Bennetts End 54 B1
Benson 13 G5
Bentley Essex 55 G2
Bentley W.Mid. 56 C3
Bentley Warks. 57 F3
Bentley Heath
Herts. 54 D2
Bentley Heath
W.Mid. 57 E5
Beoley 56 D6
Bere Alston 4 C5
Bere Ferrers 4 C5
Bere Regis 6 C5
Berinsfield 13 G5
Berkeley 12 B5
Berkhamsted 14 A4
Berkhamsted 54 A1
Berkswell 57 F5
Bermondsey 55 E4
Berners Roding 55 H1
Bernisdale 38 B3
Berriedale 43 G4
Berrow 5 G1
Berry Hill 12 B4
Berry's Green 55 F6
Berwick-upon-Tweed 33 G3
Bescar 58 B1
Bescot 56 D3
Besses o' th' Barn 59 G2
Beswick 25 E2
Betchworth 54 D6
Bethersden 9 F3
Bethesda 16 C2
Bethnal Green 55 E3
Betsham 55 H4
Bettws Bridgend 11 G5
Bettws Newport 11 H5
Bettyhill 43 E2
Betws (Y Betws) 11 E4
Betws-y-Coed 16 D3
Beulah 11 G2
Beverley 25 E3
Bewdley 12 C1
Bewdley 56 A5
Bexhill 9 E5
Bexley 55 F4
Bexleyheath 55 F4
Bicester 13 G3
Bickenhill 18 D5
Bickenhill 57 E4
Bickershaw 59 E2
Bickerstaffe 58 C2
Bickford 56 B1
Bickley 55 F5
Bicknacre 15 E4
Bicton 17 G5
Biddenden 9 E4
Biddulph 18 B2
Biddulph Moor 18 C2
Bideford 4 C2
Bidford-on-Avon 12 D2
Bidston 58 A3
Bierton 13 H4
Biggar 32 B4
Biggin Hill 8 C3
Biggin Hill 55 F6

Biggleswade 14 B2
Bilbrook 56 B2
Billericay 14 D5
Billericay 55 H2
Billinge 22 D5
Billinge 58 D3
Billingham 29 E4
Billinghay 20 A2
Billingshurst 8 A4
Billingsley 56 A4
Billington 23 E3
Billy Row 28 D4
Bilsthorpe 24 C6
Bilston Midloth. 32 C2
Bilston W.Mid. 56 C3
Bilstone 57 G2
Bilton E.Riding 25 F3
Bilton Warks. 57 H5
Binfield 13 H6
Bingham 19 G3
Bingley 23 A3
Binley 57 G5
Birch 59 G2
Birch Heath 58 D6
Birchanger 14 D3
Birchgrove 11 F5
Birchington 15 G6
Birchmoor 57 F2
Birchwood 59 E3
Bircotes 24 C5
Birdham 7 H5
Birdingbury 57 H6
Birds Green 55 G1
Birdsgreen 56 A4
Birdwell 24 B4
Birkdale 58 B1
Birkenhead 22 C5
Birkenhead 58 B4
Birling 55 H5
Birmingham 18 C5
Birmingham 56 D4
Birmingham International
Airport 57 E4
Birnam 36 C2
Birtle 59 G1
Birtley 28 D3
Bisham 13 H5
Bishop Auckland 28 D4
Bishop's Castle 17 G6
Bishop's Cleeve 12 D3
Bishop's Itchington 13 F2
Bishop's Tachbrook 13 F1
Bishop's Tachbrook 57 G6
Bishop's Tawton 4 D2
Bishop's Waltham 7 G4
Bishop's Wood 56 B2
Bishops Gate 54 A4
Bishopsteignton 5 F5
Bishopston 11 E5
Bishopthorpe 24 C2
Bishopton 31 G3
Bisley 8 A3
Bisley 54 A4
Bispham Green 58 C1
Bitchet Green 55 G6
Bitton 12 B6
Black Notley 15 H4
Blackbrook Leics. 57 H1
Blackbrook
Mersey. 58 D3
Blackburn Aber. 41 F5
Blackburn B'burn. 22 D3
Blackburn W.Loth. 32 B2
Blackden Heath 59 F5
Blackdown 57 G6
Blackfen 55 F4
Blackfield 7 F4
Blackford 36 B4
Blackford Bridge 59 G2
Blackfordby 57 G1
Blackhall Colliery 29 E4
Blackheath Gt.Lon. 55 E4
Blackheath W.Mid. 56 C4
Blackley 59 G2
Blackmore 14 D4
Blackmore 55 H1
Blackpool 22 C3
Blackrod 22 D4

Blackrod 59 E1
Blackwaterfoot 30 D5
Blackwell 19 E2
Blackwell 56 C5
Blacon 58 B6
Blackwood 11 H5
Blaenau Ffestiniog 16 C3
Blaenavon 11 H4
Blaen-gwrach 11 F4
Blaengwynfi 11 F5
Blagdon 6 A2
Blaguegate 58 C2
Blaina 11 H4
Blair Atholl 36 B1
Blairgowrie 36 D2
Blakebrook 56 B5
Blakedown 56 B5
Blakeley 56 B5
Blakenhall 56 C3
Blakeshall 56 B4
Blandford Camp 6 D4
Blandford Forum 6 C4
Blantyre 31 H4
Blaydon 28 D2
Blean 15 G6
Bledlow 13 H4
Bletchingley 8 C3
Bletchingley 55 E6
Bletchley 13 H3
Blewbury 13 G5
Blidworth 19 F2
Bliss Gate 56 A5
Blisworth 13 H2
Blockley 13 E3
Blofield 21 G4
Blossomfield 57 E5
Blowick 58 B1
Bloxham 13 F3
Bloxwich 56 C2
Bluewater 55 G4
Blundellsands 58 B3
Blundeston 21 H5
Bluntington 56 B5
Bluntisham 14 C1
Blymhill 56 B1
Blymhill Common 56 A1
Blymhill Lawn 56 B1
Blyth *Northumb.* 29 E1
Blyth *Notts.* 24 C5
Blyth End 57 F3
Bo'ness 32 B1
Boarhills 37 F4
Boat of Garten 40 B5
Bobbing 15 E6
Bobbington 56 B3
Bobbingworth 55 G1
Boddam 41 H3
Bodelwyddan 22 A6
Bodenham 12 B2
Bodicote 13 F3
Bodmin 3 H3
Bodymoor Heath 57 E3
Bognor Regis 8 A6
Bold Heath 58 D4
Boldon 29 E2
Bollington 23 F6
Bollington 59 H5
Bolney 8 B4
Bolsover 24 B6
Bolton 23 E4
Bolton 59 F2
Bolton upon Dearne 24 B4
Bolton-le-Sands 22 C1
Bolventor 4 B5
Bomere Heath 17 G5
Bonar Bridge 39 H1
Bonchester Bridge 33 E5
Bonehill 57 E2
Bonhill 31 G3
Boningale 56 B2
Bonnybridge 32 A1
Bonnyrigg 32 D2
Booth Green 59 H4
Boothstown 59 F2
Bootle 22 C5
Bootle 58 B3
Boots Green 59 F5
Borden 15 E6
Bordon 7 H3
Boreham 15 E4

Borehamwood 14 B5
Borehamwood 54 C2
Boreley 56 B6
Borgh (Barra)
  Na H-E.Siar 44 A9
Borgh (North Uist)
  Na H-E.Siar 44 C5
Borgue 26 D3
Borough Green 8 D3
Borough Green 55 H6
Boroughbridge 24 B1
Borrowdale 27 G5
Borth 16 C6
Borve (Borgh) 44 E2
Boscastle 4 B4
Bosham 7 H4
Bosherston 10 B5
Bosley 59 H6
Bostock Green 59 E6
Boston 20 B2
Boston Spa 24 B2
Botany Bay 55 E2
Botcheston 57 H2
Botesdale 15 F1
Bothel 27 G4
Bothenhampton 6 A5
Bothwell 32 A3
Botley 7 G4
Botley 54 A1
Bottesford 19 G3
Bottisham 14 D1
Bottom o'th'Moor 59 E1
Boughton 24 C6
Boughton Street 9 F3
Boundary 57 G1
Bourne 20 A3
Bourne End *Bucks.* 13 H5
Bourne End *Herts.* 54 B1
Bournebridge 55 G2
Bournemouth 6 D5
Bournheath 56 C5
Bournmoor 29 E3
Bournville 56 D4
**Bourton on
  Dunsmore** 57 H5
Bourton-on-the-Water
  13 E3
Boveney 54 A4
Bovey Tracey 5 A4
Bovingdon 14 A4
Bovingdon 54 B1
Bovinger 55 G1
Bovington Camp 6 C5
Bow Street 16 C6
Bowburn 29 F4
Bowdon 59 F4
Bowerhill 12 D6
Bowker's Green 58 C2
Bowness-on-Solway 27 G2
Bowness-on-Windermere
  27 H6
Box 12 C6
Boxford 15 F2
Boxgrove 8 A5
Boxmoor 54 B1
Boxted 15 F3
Boyndie 41 E2
Boyton Cross 55 H1
Bozeat 14 A2
Brabourne Lees 9 F3
Bracebridge Heath 25 E6
Brackley 13 G3
Bracknell 13 H6
Braco 36 B4
Bradfield 13 G6
Bradford 24 A3
Bradford-on-Avon 12 C6
Brading 7 G5
Bradley
  Ches.W. & C. 58 D5
Bradley *Staffs.* 56 B1
Bradley *W.Mid.* 56 C3
Bradley Fold 59 F2
Bradley Green
  Warks. 57 F2
Bradley Green
  Worcs. 56 C6
Bradmore 56 B3
Bradninch 5 F3
Bradpole 6 A5

Bradshaw 59 F1
Bradwall Green 59 F6
Bradwell 24 A5
Bradwell Waterside 15 F4
Brae 45 H3
Braemar 40 C3
Braintree 15 E3
Bramcote 57 H4
Bramford 15 G2
Bramhall 23 E5
Bramhall 59 G4
Bramham 24 B2
Bramhope 24 A2
Bramley *Hants.* 7 G2
Bramley *S.Yorks.* 24 B5
Bramley *Surr.* 8 A3
Brampton *Cambs.* 14 B1
Brampton *Cumb.* 28 A2
Brandesburton 25 F2
Brandon *Dur.* 28 D4
Brandon *Suff.* 20 D5
Brandon *Warks.* 57 H5
Bransgore 7 E5
Branson's Cross 56 D5
Branston *Lincs.* 25 E6
Branston *Staffs.* 18 D3
Brantham 15 G3
Branton 24 C4
Brassey Green 58 D6
Brasted 8 C2
Brasted Chart 55 F6
Bratton 6 D2
Braughing 14 C3
Braunston 13 G1
Braunton 4 C2
Bray 14 A6
Bray 54 A4
Brayton 24 C3
Breacleit 44 D3
Breage 3 F5
Bream 12 B4
Breanais 44 C3
Breaston 19 E3
Brechin 37 F1
Bredbury 59 H3
Brede 9 E5
Bredon 12 D3
Breightmet 59 F2
Brenchley 8 D3
Brent Knoll 6 A2
Brentford 54 C4
Brentwood 14 D5
Brentwood 55 G2
Brereton 56 D1
Brereton Green 59 F6
Brereton Heath 59 G6
Breretonhill 56 D1
Bretford 57 H5
Bretton 58 B6
Brewood 18 B4
Brewood 56 B2
Brickendon 55 E1
Bricket Wood 54 C1
Bridestones 59 H6
Bridge 9 G3
Bridge Trafford 58 C5
Bridge of Allan 32 A1
Bridge of Cally 36 D2
Bridge of Don 41 G5
Bridge of Earn 36 D4
Bridge of Orchy (Drochaid
  Urchaidh) 35 H3
Bridge of Weir 31 G3
Bridgend 30 B3
Bridgend (Pen-y-bont ar
  Ogwr) 11 G6
Bridgnorth 18 B5
Bridgnorth 56 A3
Bridgtown 56 C2
Bridgwater 5 G2
Bridlington 25 F1
Bridport 6 A5
Brierfield 23 E3
Brierley 24 B4
Brierley Hill 56 C4
Brig o'Turk 31 H1
Brigg 25 E4
Brighouse 24 A3

Brighstone 7 F5
Brightlingsea 15 F4
Brighton 8 C5
Brigstock 19 H5
Brill 13 G4
Brimington 24 B6
Brimscombe 12 C4
Brimstage 58 B4
Brineton 56 B1
Brinian 45 C2
Brinklow 13 F1
Brinklow 57 H5
Brinkworth 12 D5
Brinsley 19 E2
Brinsworth 24 B5
Bristol 12 B6
Briston 21 E3
Briton Ferry
  (Llansawel) 11 F5
Britwell 54 A3
Brixham 5 F6
Brixton 4 D6
Brixton 55 E4
Brixworth 13 H1
Broad Alley 56 B6
Broad Blunsdon 13 E5
Broad Green 58 D2
Broad Haven 10 A4
Broad Oak 9 E5
Broadbottom 59 H3
Broadbridge Heath 8 B4
Broadclyst 5 F4
Broadford (An t-Ath
  Leathann) 38 C4
Broadheath 59 F4
Bradley 59 G1
Broadley Common 55 F1
Broadstairs 15 H6
Broadwaters 56 B5
Broadway 13 E3
Broadwell 57 H6
Broadwey 6 B5
Broadwindsor 6 A4
Brockenhurst 7 F4
Brockham 8 B3
Brockton *Shrop.* 56 A2
Brockton *Tel. & W.* 56 A1
Brocton 56 C1
Brodick 31 E5
Brodsworth 24 C4
Broken Cross
  Ches.E. 59 G5
Broken Cross
  Ches.W. & C. 59 E5
Bromborough 58 B4
Bromham *Bed.* 14 A2
Bromham *Wilts.* 12 D6
Bromley 14 C6
Bromley 15 F5
Bromley Cross 59 F1
Brompton 29 E6
Brompton on Swale 28 D5
Bromsgrove 12 D1
Bromsgrove 56 C5
Bromstead Heath 56 B1
Bromyard 12 B2
Brondesbury 54 D3
Brook Bottom 59 H2
Brook Street 55 G2
Brooke 21 F5
Brookhouse 59 H5
Brookhouse Green 59 G6
Brookmans Park 54 D1
Brookwood 54 A6
Broom Hill 56 C5
Broome 56 C5
Broomedge 59 F4
Brora 43 F5
Broseley 18 A4
Brotton 29 F4
Brough *Cumb.* 28 B5
Brough *E.Riding* 25 E3
Brough *Shet.* 45 J3
Broughton *Flints.* 22 C6
Broughton *N.Lincs.* 25 E4
Broughton
  N.N'hants. 13 H1
Broughton Astley 19 F3
Broughton Green 56 C6

Broughton in
  Furness 27 G6
Brown Edge 18 C5
Brown Edge 58 B1
Brown Heath 58 C6
Brownhills 18 C4
Brownhills 56 D2
Brownlow 59 G6
Brownlow Heath 59 G6
Brownshill Green 57 G4
Broxbourne 55 E1
Broxburn 32 B3
Bruera 58 C6
Brundall 21 G4
Bruton 6 B3
Brymbo 17 F3
Bryn *Ches.W. & C.* 59 E5
Bryn *Gt.Man.* 58 D2
Bryn Gates 58 D2
Bryn-coch 11 F5
Brynaman 11 F4
Bryn-mawr 11 H4
Bubbenhall 57 G5
Buckden 14 B1
Buckfastleigh 5 E5
Buckhurst Hill 55 F2
Buckhaven 32 D1
Buckie 40 D2
Buckingham 13 G3
Buckland 54 D6
Buckland Common 54 A1
Buckley (Bwcle) 22 B6
Buckley *(Bwcle)* 58 A6
Buckley Green 57 E6
Bucklow Hill 59 F4
Buckridge 56 A5
Bucks Hill 54 B1
Buckton Vale 23 F4
Buckton Vale 59 H2
Budbrooke 57 F6
Bude 4 B3
Budleigh Salterton 5 F4
Budworth Heath 59 E5
Bugbrooke 13 G2
Buglawton 59 G6
Bugle 3 H4
Builth Wells (Llanfair-ym-
  Mualt) 11 G2
Bulford 7 E2
Bulkington 19 E5
Bulkington 57 G4
Bullen's Green 54 D1
Bulls Cross 55 E2
Bulphan 55 H3
Bumble's Green 55 F1
Bunbury 18 A2
Bunessan 34 C3
Bungay 21 G5
Buntingford 14 C3
Burbage *Leics.* 57 H3
Burbage *Wilts.* 13 E6
Burcot 56 C5
Burford 13 E4
Burgess Hill 8 C5
Burgh Heath 54 D6
Burgh le Marsh 25 H6
Burghclere 13 F6
Burghead 40 C2
Burghfield 13 G6
Burghfield Common 13 G6
Burghill 12 A2
Burham 15 E6
Burleigh 54 A5
Burley 7 F4
Burley in Wharfedale 24 A2
Burnage 59 G3
Burnaston 18 D3
Burnden 59 F2
Burnedge 59 H1
Burnham 14 A5
Burnham 54 A4
Burnham-on-Crouch 15 F5
Burnham-on-Sea 6 A2
Burnhaven 41 H3
Burnhill Green 56 A2
Burnhope 28 D3
Burniston 29 H6
Burnley 23 E3
Burnopfield 28 D3
Burnt Oak 54 D2

Burntcliff Top 59 H6
Burntisland 32 C1
Burntwood 56 D2
Burntwood 18 C4
Burntwood Green 56 D2
Burpham 54 B6
Burravoe 45 J2
Burrelton 36 D3
Burringham 24 D4
Burrowhill 54 A5
Burry Port 10 D4
Burscough 22 C4
Burscough 58 C1
Burscough Bridge 22 C4
Burscough Bridge 58 C1
Bursledon 7 F4
Burstwick 25 F3
Burton 7 E5
Burton (Neston) 58 B5
Burton (Tarporley) 58 D6
Burton Green 57 F5
Burton Hastings 57 H4
Burton Joyce 19 F2
Burton Latimer 14 A1
Burton upon Stather 24 D4
Burton upon Trent 18 D3
Burton-in-Kendal 22 D1
Burtonwood 22 D5
Burtonwood 58 D3
Burwash 8 D4
Burwell 14 D1
Burwick 45 C4
Bury 23 E4
Bury 59 G1
Bury St. Edmunds 15 E1
Bushbury 56 C2
Bushey 14 B5
Bushey C2
Bushey Heath 54 C2
Bussage 12 C4
Butley Town 59 H5
Buttermere 27 G5
Buttonbridge 56 A5
Buttonoak 56 A5
Buxted 8 D4
Buxton 23 F6
Byfield 13 G2
Byfleet 54 B5
Byley 59 F6

C

Cabrach 40 D4
Caddington 14 A4
Cadeby 57 H2
Cadishead 59 F3
Cadnam 7 E4
Cadole 58 A6
Caergwrle 17 G3
Caerleon 12 A5
Caernarfon 16 B2
Caerphilly 11 H5
Caer-went 12 A5
Cairnbaan 30 D2
Cairndow 31 F1
Cairneyhill 32 B1
Cairnryan 26 A2
Caister-on-Sea 21 H4
Caistor 25 F4
Cakebole 56 B5
Caldbeck 27 H4
Caldecote 57 G3
Calderbrook 59 H1
Caldercruix 32 A2
Caldicot 12 A5
Caldwell 57 F1
Caldy 58 A4
Callander 31 H1
Callington 4 C5
**Callow Hill
(Bewdley) 56 A5**
**Callow Hill
(Redditch) 56 D6**
Calne 12 D6
Calow 24 B6
Calstock 4 C5
Calver 24 A6
Calverton 19 F2
Cam 12 C5
Camberley 13 H6

Camberwell 55 E4
Camborne 3 F4
Cambourne 14 C2
Cambridge 14 C2
Camelford 4 B4
Camer 55 H5
Cammachmore 41 G6
Camp Hill 57 G3
Campbeltown (Ceann Loch
Chille Chiarain) 30 D6
Campton 14 B3
Camserney 36 B2
Canewdon 15 E5
Canisbay 43 H2
Canley 57 G5
Cannich (Canaich) 39 G4
Cannington 5 G2
Cannock 18 C4
Cannock 56 C2
Cannock Wood 56 D1
Canterbury 9 G3
Canvey Island 15 E5
Canwell Hall 57 E2
Caol 35 G1
Capel Curig 16 D3
Capel St. Mary 15 F3
Capel le Ferne 9 G4
Capenhurst 58 B5
Cappercleuch 32 C4
Caputh 36 C2
Carbost 38 B4
Carcroft 24 B4
Cardenden 32 C1
Cardiff (Caerdydd) 11 H6
Cardigan (Aberteifi) 10 C2
Carharrack 3 G4
Carinish (Cairinis) 44 B6
Carlisle 27 H3
Carloway
(Càrlabhagh) 44 D2
Carlton Leics. 57 G2
Carlton N.Yorks. 24 C3
Carlton Notts. 19 F2
Carlton Colville 21 H5
Carlton Miniott 29 E6
Carlton in Lindrick 24 C5
Carluke 32 A3
Carlyon Bay 3 H4
Carmarthen
(Caerfyrddin) 10 D4
Carnbo 36 C4
Carnforth 22 C1
Carno 17 E6
Carnoustie 37 F3
Carnwath 32 B3
Carol Green 57 F5
Carr Houses 58 B2
Carradale 30 D5
Carrbridge 40 B4
Carrington 59 F3
Carshalton 54 D5
**Carshalton
Beeches 54 D5**
Carsphairn 26 D1
Carterton 13 E4
Cartmel 22 C1
Castle Bromwich 57 E4
Castle Cary 6 B3
Castle Donington 19 E3
Castle Douglas 27 E2
Castle End 57 F5
Castle Green 54 A5
Castle Gresley 57 F1
Castle Hedingham 15 E3
Castle Kennedy 26 B3
Castlebay (Bàgh a' Chaisteil)
44 A10
Castleford 24 B3
Castlemartin 10 B5
Castleton 59 G1
Castletown High. 43 G2
Castletown I.o.M. 26 B6
Caterham 8 C3
Caterham 55 E6
Catford 55 E4
**Catherine-de-Barnes
57 E4**
Caton 22 D1

Camberwell 55 E4
Catrine 31 H5
Catshill 12 D1
Catshill 56 C5
Catterall 22 C2
Catterick 28 D6
Catterick Garrison 28 D6
Catterline 37 G1
Catton Hall 57 F1
Caunsall 56 B4
Causeway End 58 C1
Caverswall 18 C2
Cawdor 40 A3
Cawood 24 C3
Cawston Norf. 21 F3
Cawston Warks. 57 H5
Caythorpe 19 H2
Cayton 29 H6
Ceann a' Bhàigh 44 B6
Cearsiadair 44 E4
Cefn-mawr 17 F3
Cemaes 16 B1
Ceres 37 E4
Chad Valley 56 D4
Chadderton 23 F4
Chadderton 59 H2
Chadderton Fold 59 G2
Chaddesley Corbett 12 C1
Chaddesley Corbett 56 B5
Chadwell 56 A1
Chadwell Heath 55 F3
Chadwell St. Mary 14 D6
Chadwell St. Mary 55 H4
Chadwick End 57 F5
Chafford Hundred 55 H4
Chagford 5 E4
Chaldon 55 E6
Chalfont Common 54 B2
Chalfont St. Giles 14 A5
Chalfont St. Giles 54 A5
Chalfont St. Peter 14 A5
Chalfont St. Peter 54 B2
Chalford 12 C4
Chalgrove 13 G5
Chalk 55 H4
Chalvey 54 A4
Chandler's Cross 54 B2
**Chapel Green
(Fillongley) 57 F4**
**Chapel Green
(Southam) 57 H6**
Chapel St. Leonards 25 H6
Chapel of Garioch 41 F4
Chapel-en-le-Frith 23 F5
Chapelhall 32 A2
Chapeltown B'burn. 23 E4
**Chapeltown
B'burn. 59 F1**
Chapeltown S.Yorks. 24 B5
Chard 6 A4
Chardstock 6 A4
Charfield 12 C5
Charing 9 F3
Charlbury 13 F4
Charleston 37 E2
**Charlestown
Gt.Man. 59 G2**
Charlestown High. 38 D2
Charlesworth 23 F5
Charlton 55 F4
Charlton Down 6 B5
Charlwood 8 B3
Charminster 6 B5
Charmouth 6 A5
Charnock Richard 22 D4
Charnock Richard 58 D1
Chartham 9 G3
Chartridge 54 A1
Charvil 13 H4
Chase Terrace 56 D2
Chasetown 56 D2
Chatham 15 E5
Chatteris 20 B5
Cheadle Gt.Man. 23 G5
Cheadle Gt.Man. 59 G4
Cheadle Staffs. 18 C2
Cheadle Heath 59 G4
Cheadle Hulme 59 G4
Cheam 54 D5
Cheapside 54 A5
Cheddar 6 A2

Cheddington 14 A4
Cheddleton 18 C2
Chedgrave 21 G5
Cheesden 59 G1
Cheetham Hill 59 G2
Chelford 59 G5
Chelmarsh 56 A4
Chelmondiston 15 G3
Chelmsford 15 E4
Chelmsley Wood 57 E4
Chelsea 54 D4
Chelsfield 55 F5
Chelsham 55 E6
Cheltenham 12 D3
Chenies 54 B2
Chepstow
(Cas-gwent) 12 B5
Cherry Burton 25 E2
Cherry Willingham 25 E6
Chertsey 14 A6
Chertsey 54 B5
Chesham 14 A4
Chesham 54 A1
Chesham Bois 54 A1
Cheshunt 14 C4
Cheshunt 55 E1
Cheslyn Hay 18 C4
Cheslyn Hay 56 C2
Chessington 54 C5
Chestall 56 D1
Chester 22 C6
Chester 58 C6
Chester-le-Street 28 D3
Chesterfield Derbys. 24 B6
Chesterfield Staffs. 57 E2
Chesterton 13 G3
Chesterton 56 A3
Cheswardine 18 B3
Cheswick Green 13 E1
Cheswick Green 57 E5
Chetwynd Aston 56 A1
Cheveley 14 D1
Chevening 55 F6
Chew Magna 12 B6
Chew Moor 59 E2
Chichester 7 H4
Chickerell 6 B5
Chicksands 14 B3
Chiddingfold 8 A4
Chieveley 13 F6
**Chignall St. James
55 H1**
Chigwell 14 C5
Chigwell 55 F2
Chigwell Row 55 F2
Chilcompton 6 B2
Chilcote 57 F1
Childer Thornton 58 B5
Childerditch 55 H3
Childs Hill 54 D3
Childwall 58 C4
Chilham 9 F3
Chilton 28 D4
Chilvers Coton 57 G3
Chingford 55 E2
Chinnor 13 H4
Chippenham 12 D6
Chipperfield 54 B1
Chipping Campden 13 E3
Chipping Norton 13 F3
Chipping Ongar 14 D4
Chipping Ongar 55 G1
Chipping Sodbury 12 C5
Chipstead Kent 55 F6
Chipstead Surr. 54 D6
Chirk (Y Waun) 17 F4
Chirnside 33 F3
Chiseldon 13 E5
Chislehurst 55 F4
Chiswick 54 D4
Chiswick Green 54 C1
Chisworth 59 H3
Chobham 54 A5
Cholesbury 54 A1
Cholsey 13 G5
Chopwell 28 D3
Chorley Lancs. 22 D4
Chorley Lancs. 58 D1
Chorley Staffs. 56 D1
Chorleywood 14 A5
Chorleywood 54 B2

**Chorlton-cum-Hardy
59 G3**
Christchurch 7 E5
Christleton 58 C6
Chryston 31 H3
Chudleigh 5 E4
Chulmleigh 4 D3
Church Aston 18 B4
Church Aston 56 A1
Church Eaton 56 B1
Church End 57 F3
Church Gresley 57 F1
Church Hill 59 E6
Church Langley 55 F1
Church Lawford 57 H5
Church Minshull 59 E6
Church Stretton 17 G6
**Church Town
Leics. 57 G1**
Church Town Surr. 55 E6
Church Village 11 G5
Churchdown 12 C3
Churchfield 56 D3
Churchgate 55 E1
Churchill 6 A2
Churchill 56 B5
Churchtown 58 B1
Cilcain 22 B6
Cinderford 12 B4
Cippenham 54 A3
Cirencester 12 D4
City 55 E3
City Airport 55 F3
Clackmannan 32 B1
Clacton-on-Sea 15 G4
Clanfield 13 E4
Claonaig 30 D4
Clapham Bed. 14 A2
Clapham Gt.Lon. 54 D4
Clarborough 24 D5
Clare 15 E2
Clashmore 40 A1
Clatterford End 55 G1
Claverdon 13 E1
Claverdon 57 E6
Clavering 14 C3
Claverley 18 B5
Claverley 56 A3
Clay Cross 24 B6
Claybrooke Magna 57 H4
Claybrooke Parva 57 H4
Claydon 15 G2
Claygate 54 C5
Claygate Cross 55 H6
Clayhanger 56 D2
Clayton West 24 A4
Clayton-le-Moors 23 E3
Cleator Moor 27 F5
Cleckheaton 24 A3
Cleethorpes 25 G4
Clehonger 12 A3
Clenchwarton 20 C3
Clent 12 D1
Clent 56 C5
Cleobury Mortimer 12 B1
Clevedon 12 A6
Cleveleys 22 C2
Clewer Green 54 A4
Clewer Village 54 A4
Cliffe 15 E6
Cliffe Woods 15 E6
Clifton 14 B3
Clifton Campville 57 F1
Clifton upon
Dunsmore 13 G1
Clifton upon Teme 56 A6
Clipstone 24 C6
Clitheroe 23 E2
Clochan 40 D2
Clock Face 58 D3
Clola 41 G3
Clophill 14 A3
Clotton 58 D6
Clough
(Littleborough) 59 H1
Clough (Shaw) 59 H2
Clova 37 E1
Clovelly 4 C2
Clowne 24 B6
Clows Top 56 A5

Clun 17 F6
Clunderwen 10 C4
Clutton 6 B2
Clydach 11 E4
Clydach Vale 11 G5
Clydebank 31 H3
Coalburn 32 A4
Coalport 56 A2
Coalville 19 E4
Coalville 57 H1
Coatbridge 32 A2
Coates 20 B5
Cobham Kent 55 H5
Cobham Surr. 8 B3
Cobham Surr. 54 C5
Cobley Hill 56 D5
Cockenzie and
    Port Seton 32 D2
Cockermouth 27 G4
Cockfield 28 D4
Cockfosters 54 D2
Coddington 19 G2
Codicote 14 B4
Codnor 19 E2
Codsall 18 B4
Codsall 56 B2
Codsall Wood 56 B2
Coed-poeth 17 F3
Cofton Hackett 12 D1
Cofton Hackett 56 D5
Coggeshall 15 E3
Colburn 28 D6
Colchester 15 F3
Cold Ash 13 G6
Coldblow 55 G4
Colden Common 7 F3
Coldstream 33 F4
Cole End 57 E4
Coleford Glos. 12 B6
Coleford Som. 6 B2
Colehill 6 D4
Colemore Green 56 A3
Coleorton 57 H1
Colerne 12 B6
Coleshill Bucks. 54 A2
Coleshill Warks. 18 D5
Coleshill Warks. 57 F4
Colindale 54 B4
Colinsburgh 37 E4
Colintraive 31 E3
Collier Row 55 G2
Collier's Wood 54 D4
Collieston 41 G4
Collingham Notts. 24 D6
Collingham W.Yorks. 24 B2
Collins Green 58 D3
Colliston 37 F2
Collycroft 57 G4
Collyhurst 59 G2
Colnbrook 14 A6
Colnbrook 54 B4
Colne Cambs. 14 C1
Colne Lancs. 23 E2
Colney Heath 14 B4
Colney Heath 54 D1
Colney Street 54 C1
Colsterworth 19 H3
Coltishall 21 F4
Colwich 18 C3
Colwyn Bay
    (Bae Colwyn) 16 D2
Colyton 5 G4
Combe Martin 4 D1
Combe St. Nicholas 6 A4
Comberbach 59 E5
Comberford 57 E2
Comberton 14 C2
Comhampton 56 B6
Compstall 59 H3
Compton Hants. 7 F3
Compton Staffs. 56 B4
Compton W.Berks. 13 G6
Comrie 36 B3
Condover 17 G5
Congerstone 57 G2
Congleton 23 E6
Congleton 59 G6
Congresbury 12 A6
Congreve 56 C1
Coningsby 20 A2

Conisbrough 24 C5
Coniston 27 H6
Connah's Quay 22 B6
Connah's Quay 58 A6
Connel
    (A' Choingheal) 35 F3
Conon Bridge (Drochaid
    Sgùideil) 39 H3
Consett 28 D3
Constantine 3 G5
Contin (Cunndainn) 39 G3
Conwy 16 D2
Cookham 13 H5
Cookley 18 B5
Cookley 56 B4
Cooksey Green 56 C6
Cooksmill Green 55 H1
Cooper's Green 54 C1
Coopersale 55 F1
Coopersale Street 55 F1
Copmanthorpe 24 C2
Coppenhall 56 C1
Coppicegate 56 A4
Coppull 22 D4
Coppull 58 D1
Coppull Moor 58 D1
Copse Hill 54 D5
Copston Magna 57 H4
Copt Heath 57 E5
Copt Oak 57 H1
Copthall Green 55 F1
Copthorne 8 C4
Copythorne 7 F4
Corbets Tey 55 G3
Corbridge 28 C2
Corby 19 H5
Corfe Castle 6 D5
Corfe Mullen 6 D5
Corley 57 G4
Corley Ash 57 F4
Corley Moor 57 F4
Cornforth 29 E4
Cornhill 41 E3
Cornhill on Tweed 33 F4
Corpach
    (A' Chorpaich) 35 F1
Corran (Ardgour) 35 F1
Corringham 15 E5
Corsham 12 C6
Corton 21 H5
Corwen 17 E3
Cosby 19 F5
Coseley 56 C3
Cosford 56 A2
Costessey 21 F4
Cotebrook 58 D6
Cotgrave 19 F3
Coton 57 G2
Coton in the Elms 57 F1
Cottenham 14 C1
Cotteridge 56 D5
Cottesmore 19 H4
Cottingham E.Riding 25 E3
Cottingham
    N.N'hants. 19 G5
Coughton 56 D6
Coulsdon 54 D6
Coundon Dur. 28 D4
Coundon W.Mid. 57 G4
Countesthorpe 19 F5
Coupar Angus 36 D2
Court House Green 57 G4
Cove Bay 41 G5
Coven 18 C4
Coven 56 C2
Coventry 13 F1
Coventry 57 G5
Coventry Airport 57 G5
Cowbridge 11 G6
Cowdenbeath 32 C1
Cowes 7 F5
Cowfold 8 B4
Cowie Aber. 41 F6
Cowie Stir. 32 A1
Cowley 54 B3
Cowling Lancs. 58 D1
Cowling N.Yorks. 23 F2
Coxheath 9 E3
Coxhoe 29 E4
Coxtie Green 55 G2

Coychurch 11 G6
Coylton 31 G6
Crackleybank 56 A1
Cradley Here. 12 C2
Cradley W.Mid. 56 C4
Cradley Heath 56 C4
Craigellachie 40 C3
Craighouse 30 C3
Craignure 35 E3
Craigo 37 F1
Craigrothie 37 E4
Craigton (Monikie)
    Angus 37 F3
Craigton (by Kirriemuir)
    Angus 37 E2
Crail 37 F4
Cramlington 28 D2
Cranage 59 F6
Cranbourne 54 A4
Cranbrook 9 E4
Cranbrook 55 F3
Cranfield 14 A2
Cranford 54 C4
Cranham 55 G3
Crank 58 D3
Cranleigh 8 A4
Cranwell 19 H2
Crateford 56 C2
Crathes 41 F6
Craven Arms 17 G6
Crawcrook 28 D2
Crawford 58 C2
Crawley 8 B4
Crawley Down 8 C4
Crayford 55 G4
Credenhill 12 A2
Crediton 5 E3
Creech St. Michael 5 G2
Creekmouth 55 F3
Creswell 24 C6
Crewe 18 B2
Crewkerne 6 A4
Crianlarich (A' Chrìon-
    Làraich) 35 H3
Criccieth 16 C4
Crick 13 G1
Crickhowell 11 H4
Cricklade 12 D5
Cricklewood 54 D3
Crieff 36 B3
Crigglestone 24 B4
Crimble 59 G1
Crimond 41 G3
Crinan 30 D2
Cringleford 21 F4
Crockenhill 55 G5
Crocketford or
    Ninemile Bar 27 E2
Crockham Hill 55 F6
Croeserw 11 F5
Croft 59 E3
Crofton 24 B4
Croggan 35 E3
Cromarty (Cromba) 40 A2
Cromdale 40 B4
Cromer 21 F2
Cromford 18 D2
Cromhall 12 B5
Cromore 44 E3
Crompton Fold 59 H1
Crondall 7 H2
Cronton 22 C5
Cronton 58 C4
Crook 28 D4
Crook of Devon 36 C4
Crookham 33 G4
Crosbost 44 E5
Crosby 22 C5
Crosby 58 B3
Cross Bank 56 A5
Cross Green 56 C2
Cross Hands 11 E4
Cross Lane Head 56 A3
Crossens 58 B1
Crossford 32 B1
Crossgates Fife 32 C1
Crossgates Powys 11 G1
Crosshouse 31 G5
Crossmichael 27 E2
Crossway Green 56 B6

Crossways 6 C5
Croston 22 C4
Croston 58 C1
Crouch 55 H6
Crouch End 54 D3
Croughton 13 G3
Crovie 41 F2
Crow Green 55 G2
Crowborough 8 D4
Crowland 20 A4
Crowle 24 D4
Crowthorne 13 H6
Crowton 58 D5
Croxall 57 F1
Croxley Green 54 B2
Croy 40 A3
Croyde 4 C2
Croydon 14 D3
Croydon 55 E5
Cruden Bay 41 G4
Crumlin 11 H5
Crumpsall 59 G2
Crynant 11 F4
Crystal Palace 55 E4
Cubbington 13 F1
Cubbington 57 G6
Cuckfield 8 C4
Cuckoo's Nest 58 B6
Cuddington 22 D6
Cuddington 58 D5
Cudham 55 F6
Cudworth 24 B4
Cuerdley Cross 58 D4
Cuffley 14 C4
Cuffley 55 E1
Culbokie
    (Cùil Bhàicidh) 39 H3
Culcheth 22 D5
Culcheth 59 E3
Culkein 42 A4
Cullen 41 D2
Cullingworth 23 F3
Cullipool 30 D1
Cullivoe 45 J1
Culloden 40 A3
Cullompton 5 F3
Culverstone Green 55 H5
Cumbernauld 32 A2
Cuminestown 41 F3
Cummingstown 40 C2
Cumnock 31 H5
Cumnor 13 F4
Cunningsburgh 45 H5
Cupar 37 E4
Curborough 57 E1
Curdridge 7 G4
Curdworth 57 E3
Curry Rivel 6 A3
Cutgate 59 G1
Cutnall Green 56 B6
Cuxton 15 E6
Cwm 11 H4
Cwmafan 11 F5
Cwmbach 11 G4
Cwmbrân 11 H5
Cwmllynfell 11 F4
Cymmer 11 G5

D

Dadlington 57 H3
Dagenham 55 F3
Dairsie (Osnaburgh) 37 E4
Daisy Bank 56 D3
Dalabrog 44 B8
Dalavich 31 E1
Dalbeattie 27 E2
Dale Gt.Man. 59 H2
Dale Pembs. 10 A4
Dalgety Bay 32 C1
Dalhalvaig 43 F3
Dalkeith 32 D2
Dallas 40 C3
Dalmally
    (Dail Mhàilidh) 35 G3
Dalmellington 31 G6
Dalry 31 F4
Dalrymple 31 G6
Dalston 27 H3

Dalton Lancs. 58 C2
Dalton S.Yorks. 24 B5
Dalton-in-Furness 22 B1
Dalwhinnie 39 H6
Danbury 15 E4
Dancers Hill 54 D2
Danderhall 32 D2
Dane Bank 59 H3
Danebridge 59 H6
Danehill 8 C4
Danzey Green 57 E6
Darby End 56 C4
Darenth 14 D6
Darenth 55 G4
Daresbury 58 D4
Darfield 24 B4
Darlaston 56 C3
Darley Dale 24 A6
Darlington 28 D5
Dartford 14 D6
Dartford 55 G4
Dartington 5 E5
Dartmouth 5 E6
Darton 24 B4
Darvel 31 H5
Darwen 22 D3
Datchet 54 A4
Daubhill 59 E2
Davenham 22 D6
Davenham 59 E5
Davenport Green 59 G4
Daventry 13 G1
Daviot 41 E3
Davyhulme 59 F3
Dawlish 5 F5
Dayhouse Bank 56 C5
Deal 9 H3
Dean Row 59 G4
Deane 59 E2
Deansgreen 59 E4
Deanshanger 13 H3
Deanston 36 B4
Dearham 27 F4
Debden Green 55 F2
Debenham 15 G1
Decker Hill 56 A1
Deddington 13 F3
Dedham 15 F3
Dedworth 54 A4
Deepcut 54 B4
Deeping St. James 20 A4
Deeping St. Nicholas 20 A4
Deiniolen 16 C2
Delamere 22 D6
Delamere 58 D6
Delph 23 F4
Delph 59 H2
Denbigh (Dinbych) 22 A6
Denby Dale 24 A4
Denham 14 A5
Denham 58 B3
Denham Green 54 B3
Denholm 33 E5
Denholme 23 F3
Denmead 7 G4
Denny 32 A1
Denshaw 59 H1
Denton Gt.Man. 23 F5
Denton Gt.Man. 59 H3
Denton Kent 55 H4
Denton's Green 58 C3
Deptford 55 E4
Derby 19 E3
Dereham
    (East Dereham) 21 E4
Dersingham 20 C3
Dervaig 34 C2
Desborough 19 G5
Desford 19 E4
Desford 57 H2
Devil's Bridge
    Pontarfynach 11 F1
Devitts Green 57 F3
Devizes 12 D6
Dewsbury 24 A3
Dibden 7 F4
Dibden Hill 54 A2
Didcot 13 G5
Didsbury 59 G3
Digmoor 58 C2

Dilton Marsh 6 C2
Dimple 59 F1
Dinas Powys 11 H6
Dinas Mawddwy 16 D5
Dingwall (Inbhir Pheofharain)
   39 H3
Dinnington *S.Yorks.* 24 C5
Dinnington *T. & W.* 28 D2
Disley 23 F5
Disley 59 H4
Diss 21 F5
Distington 27 F4
Ditchingham 21 G5
Ditchling 8 C5
Ditton *Halton* 58 C4
Ditton *Kent* 9 E3
Dobcross 59 H2
Dobwalls 4 B5
Docking 20 D3
Doddington 14 D5
Doddinghurst 55 G2
Doddington 20 B5
Dodford 56 C5
Dodleston 58 B6
Dodworth 24 B4
Doffcocker 59 E1
Dolgellau 16 D5
Dollar 32 B1
Doncaster 24 C4
Donington *Lincs.* 20 A3
Donington *Shrop.* 56 B2
Donington le
  Heath 57 H1
Donisthorpe 19 E4
Donistorpe 57 G1
Donnington 56 A1
Dorchester *Dorset* 6 B5
Dorchester *Oxon.* 13 G5
Dordon 18 D4
Dordon 57 F2
Dores (Duras) 39 H4
Dorking 8 B3
Dormer's Wells 54 C3
Dorney 54 A4
Dorney Reach 54 A4
Dornie (An Dòrnaidh) 38 D4
Dornoch 40 A1
Dorridge 57 E5
Dosthill 57 F3
Douglas *I.o.M.* 26 C6
Douglas *S.Lan.* 32 A4
Dounby 45 B2
Doune 36 B4
Dover 9 H3
Doverdale 56 B6
Doveridge 18 D3
Downe 55 F5
Downham Market 20 C4
Downholland Cross 58 B2
Downside 54 C6
Downton 7 E3
Drakelow 56 B4
Drakes Cross 56 D5
Draycote 57 H6
Draycott 56 B3
Draycott in the
  Moors 18 C3
Drayton *Worcs.* 56 C5
Drayton Bassett 57 E2
Dreghorn 31 G5
Driffield 25 E2
Droitwich 12 C1
Droitwich Spa 56 B6
Dronfield 24 B6
Drongan 31 G6
Dropmore 54 A3
Droylsden 23 F5
Droylsden 59 H3
Drumbeg 42 B4
Drumlithie 41 F6
Drummore 26 B4
Drumnadrochit (Druim na
  Drochaid) 39 H4
Drumoak 41 F6
Drury 58 A6
Dry Street 55 H3
Drybrook 12 B4
Ducklington 13 F4
Ducks Island 54 D2

Duddon 58 D6
Dudley *T. & W.* 28 D2
Dudley *W.Mid.* 18 C5
Dudley *W.Mid.* 56 C3
Dudley Port 56 C3
Dudlow's Green 59 E4
Duffield 19 E2
Dufftown 40 D3
Duffus 40 C2
Duke End 57 F4
Dukinfield 23 F5
Dukinfield 59 H3
Dull 36 B2
Dulnain Bridge 40 B4
Dulverton 5 F2
Dulwich 55 E4
Dumbarton 31 G3
Dumfries 27 F2
Dunbar 33 E2
Dunbeath 43 G4
Dunbeg
  (An Dùn Beag) 35 E3
Dunblane 36 B4
Dunchurch 13 F1
Dunchurch 57 H5
Dundee 37 E3
Dundonald 31 G5
Dunecht 41 F5
Dunfermline 32 B1
Dunham Town 59 F4
Dunham
  Woodhouses 59 F4
**Dunham-on-the-Hill
  58 C5**
Dunhampton 56 B6
Dunholme 25 E6
Dunipace 32 A1
Dunk's Green 55 H6
Dunkeld 36 C2
**Dunkirk
  Ches.W. & C. 58 D7**
Dunkirk *Kent* 9 F3
Dunley 56 A6
Dunnet 43 G2
Dunning 36 C4
Dunnington 24 C2
Dunoon 31 F3
Duns 33 F3
Dunsfold 8 A4
Dunsley 56 B4
Dunstable 14 A3
Dunston 56 C1
Dunston Heath 56 C1
Dunton Green 55 G6
Dunton Wayletts 55 H2
Dunvant 11 E5
Dunvegan 38 A3
Durham 28 D3
Durness 42 C2
Durrington 7 E2
Dursley 12 C5
Duthil 40 B4
Dutton 58 D5
Duxford 14 C2
Dwygyfylchi 16 D2
Dyce 41 F5
Dyke 40 B3
Dykehead 37 E1
Dymchurch 9 F4
Dymock 12 C3
Dyserth 22 A6

E

Eaglesham 31 H4
Eagley 59 F1
Ealing 14 B5
Ealing 54 C3
Earby 23 F2
Eardington 56 A3
Earith 14 C1
Earl Shilton 19 E5
Earl Shilton 57 H3
Earl's Court 54 D4
Earlestown 58 D3
Earls Barton 13 H1
Earls Colne 15 E3
Earlsdon 57 G5
Earlston 33 E4
Earlswood 57 E5

Easebourne 7 H3
Easenhall 57 H5
Easington *Dur.* 29 E3
Easington *E.Riding* 25 G4
Easington Colliery 29 E3
Easingwold 24 C1
East Acton 54 D3
East Ayton 29 H6
East Barnet 54 D1
East Bedfont 54 B4
East Bergholt 15 F4
East Bridgford 19 F2
East Burnham 54 A3
East Calder 32 B2
East Challow 13 F5
East Clandon 54 B6
East Cowes 6 B4
East Cowes 7 G5
East Dean 8 D6
East Farleigh 9 E3
East Goscote 19 F4
East Grinstead 8 C4
East Hagbourne 13 G5
East Ham 55 F3
East Hanningfield 15 E4
East Harling 21 E5
East Hendred 13 F5
East Horndon 55 H3
East Horsley 8 A3
East Horsley 54 B6
East Huntspill 6 A2
East Kilbride 31 H4
East Leake 19 F3
East Linton 33 E2
East Malling 9 E3
East Malling Heath 55 H6
East Molesey 54 C5
East Peckham 8 D3
East Preston 8 A5
East Tilbury 55 H4
East Wemyss 32 D1
East Wickham 55 F4
East Wittering 7 H5
Eastbourne 8 D6
Eastbury 54 C2
Eastchurch 15 F6
Eastcote *Gt.Lon.* 54 C3
Eastcote *W.Mid.* 57 E5
Eastergate 8 A5
Eastfield 29 H6
Eastham 58 B4
Eastington 12 C4
Eastleigh 7 F4
Easton 6 B6
Easton on the Hill 19 H4
Easton-in-Gordano 12 B6
Eastrea 20 A5
Eastriggs 27 G2
Eastry 9 G3
Eastwood 19 E2
Eathorpe 57 G6
Eaton *Ches.E.* 59 G6
Eaton *Ches.W. & C.* 58 D6
Eaton Bray 14 A3
Eaton Hall 58 C6
Eaves Green 57 F4
Ebbsfleet Valley 55 H4
Ebbw Vale (Glyn Ebwy) 11 H4
Eccles *Gt.Man.* 23 E5
Eccles *Gt.Man.* 59 F3
Eccles *Kent* 15 E6
Eccleshall 18 B3
**Eccleston
  Ches.W. & C. 58 C6**
Eccleston *Lancs.* 22 D4
Eccleston *Lancs.* 58 D1
Eccleston *Mersey.* 58 C3
Echt 41 F5
Eckington *Derbys.* 24 B6
Eckington *Worcs.* 12 D2
Edderton 40 A1
Eden Park 55 E5
Edenbridge 8 C3
Edenfield 23 E4
Edenfield 59 F1
Edgbaston 56 D4
Edge Green 58 D3
Edgmond 18 B4
Edgmond 56 A1
Edgware 54 D2

Edgworth 23 E4
Edgworth 59 F1
Edinbane 38 B3
Edinburgh 32 C2
Edingale 57 F1
Edith Weston 19 H4
Edmonton 55 E2
Edney Common 55 H1
Edstone 57 E6
Edwinstowe 24 C6
Edzell 37 F1
Effingham 8 B2
Effingham 54 C6
Efflinch 57 E1
Egerton 23 E4
Egerton 59 F1
Eggborough 24 C3
Egham 14 A6
Egham 54 B4
Egham Wick 54 A4
Egremont 27 F5
Eight Ash Green 15 F3
Elderslie 31 G3
Elford 57 E1
Elgin 40 C2
Elgol 38 C5
Elham 9 G3
Elie 37 E4
Elland 24 A3
Ellenabeich 30 D1
Ellesmere 17 G4
Ellesmere Park 59 F3
Ellesmere Port 22 C6
Ellesmere Port 58 C5
Ellington 28 D1
Ellistown 19 E4
Ellistown 57 H1
Ellon 41 G4
Elloughton 25 E3
Elm 20 B4
Elm Park 55 G3
Elmbridge 56 C6
Elmdon 57 E4
Elmdon Heath 57 E4
Elmer's Green 58 C2
Elmers End 55 E5
Elmesthorpe 57 H3
Elmhurst 57 E1
Elmley Lovett 56 B6
Elmstead 57 F4
Elmstead Market 15 F3
Elmswell 15 F1
Elphin 42 B5
Elsenham 14 D3
Elstead 8 A3
Elstree 54 C2
Eltham 55 F4
Elton *Ches.W. & C.* 22 C6
Elton *Ches.W. & C.* 58 C5
Elton *Gt.Man.* 59 F1
Elton Green 58 C5
Elworth 23 E6
Elworth 59 F6
Ely 14 D1
Embo 40 A1
Embsay 23 F2
Emerson Park 55 G3
Emneth 20 B4
Emsworth 7 H4
Enderby 19 F5
Endon 18 C2
Enfield 14 C5
Enfield 55 E2
Enfield Wash 55 E2
Englefield Green 54 A4
Enstone 13 F3
Enville 56 B4
Eòrapaidh 44 F1
Epping 14 C4
Epping 55 F1
**Epping Green
  Essex 55 F1**
**Epping Green
  Herts. 55 D1**
Epping Upland 55 F1
Epsom 14 B6
Epsom 54 D5
Epworth 24 D4
Erdington 57 E3

Erith 55 G4
Errol 36 D3
Erskine 31 G3
Esh Winning 28 D3
Esher 14 B6
Esher 54 C5
Eskdalemuir 27 G1
Essendon 54 D1
Essington 18 C4
Essington 56 C2
Etchinghill 56 D1
Eton 14 A6
Eton 54 A4
Eton Wick 54 A4
Ettiley Heath 59 F6
Ettrick 32 C5
Etwall 18 D3
Euxton 22 D4
Euxton 58 D1
Evanton 39 H2
Evenwood 28 D4
Evercreech 6 B3
Everton 58 B3
Evesham 12 D2
Ewell 14 B6
Ewell 54 D5
Ewenny 11 G6
Ewhurst 8 A3
Ewloe 58 B6
Ewloe Green 58 A6
Exeter 5 F4
Exhall 57 G4
Exminster 5 F4
Exmouth 5 F4
Exning 14 D1
Eye *Peter.* 20 A4
Eye *Suff.* 15 G1
Eyemouth 33 G2
Eynsford 55 G5
Eynsham 13 F4
Eythorne 9 G3

F

Facit 59 G1
Failsworth 23 E4
Failsworth 59 G2
Fair Oak 7 F4
Fairfield *Gt.Man.* 59 H3
Fairfield *Mersey.* 58 A4
Fairfield *Worcs.* 56 C5
Fairford 13 E4
Fairlie 31 F4
Fairlight 9 E5
Fairmile 54 C5
Fairseat 55 H5
Fakenham 21 E3
Falkirk 32 A1
Falkland 36 D4
Fallin 32 A1
Falmouth 3 G5
Far Forest 56 A5
Far Moor 58 D2
Farcet 20 A5
Fareham 7 G4
Farewell 56 D1
Faringdon 13 E5
Farleigh 55 E5
Farm Town 57 G1
Farmborough 12 B6
**Farnborough
  Gt.Lon. 55 F5**
Farnborough
  Ches.W. & C. 17 G3
Farndon *Notts.* 19 G2
Farnell 37 F2
Farnham 7 H2
Farnham Common 54 A3
Farnham Royal 14 A5
Farnham Royal 54 A3
Farningham 55 G5
Farnsfield 19 F2
Farnworth *Gt.Man.* 23 E4
Farnworth *Gt.Man.* 59 F2
Farnworth *Halton* 58 D4
Fauldhouse 32 B2
Faversham 15 F6
Fawkham Green 55 G5
Fawley 7 F4

Fazakerley 58 B3
Fazeley 18 D4
Fazeley 57 F2
Fearnan 36 B2
Fearnhead 59 E3
Featherstone *Staffs.* 18 C4
Featherstone
  Staffs. 56 C2
Featherstone
  W.Yorks. 24 B4
Feckenham 56 D6
Feering 15 E4
Felden 54 B1
Felindre 17 F6
Felixstowe 15 H3
Felling 28 D2
Felsted 14 D3
Feltham 54 C4
Felthamhill 54 C4
Feltwell 20 D5
Fen End 57 F5
Feniton 5 G4
Fenny Drayton 57 G3
Fenstanton 14 C1
Feock 3 G5
Feolin Ferry 30 B3
Ferndale 11 G5
Ferndown 6 D4
Fernhill Heath 12 C2
Fernhurst 7 H3
Ferring 8 A5
Ferryden 37 G2
Ferryhill 28 D4
Ferryside (Glanyferi)
  10 D4
Fetcham 54 C6
Fetterangus 41 G3
Fettercairn 37 F1
Ffestiniog (Llan Ffestiniog)
  16 D3
Ffostrasol 10 D2
Fiddlers Hamlet 55 F1
Field Head 57 H2
Fifield 54 A4
Filey 25 F1
Fillongley 18 D5
Finchley 54 D2
Finchampstead 13 H6
Finchingfield 14 D3
Finchley 54 D2
Findhorn 40 B2
Findochty 40 D2
Findon *Aber.* 41 G6
Findon *W.Suss.* 8 B5
Finedon 14 A1
Fingerpost 56 A5
Finney Hill 57 H1
Finningley 24 C5
Finsbury 55 E3
Finstall 56 C5
Finstown 45 C3
Finwood 57 E6
Firgrove 59 H1
Firs Lane 59 E2
Fishburn 29 E4
Fishguard
  (Abergwaun) 10 B3
Fishnish 34 D2
Fishpool 59 G2
Fishtoft 20 B2
Fitzwilliam 24 B4
Five Oaks 5 H6
Flackwell Heath 13 H5
Flamborough 25 F1
Flamstead 14 A4
Flamstead End 55 E1
Flaunden 54 B1
Fleckney 19 F5
Fleet 7 H2
Fleetville 54 C1
Fleetwood 22 C2
Flexford 54 A6
Flimby 27 F4
Flint (Y Fflint) 22 B6
Flint (Y Fflint) 58 A5
Flint Mountain 58 A5
Flint's Green 57 F4
Flitwick 14 A3
Flixton 59 F3

Flore 13 G1
Fochabers 40 D3
Fodderty 39 H3
Foleshill 57 G4
Folkestone 9 G4
Footherley 57 E2
Foots Cray 55 F4
Force Green 55 F6
Ford *Arg. & B.* 30 D1
Ford *Mersey.* 58 B3
Fordbridge 57 E4
Fordham 14 D1
Fordhouses 56 C2
Fordingbridge 7 E4
Fordoun 37 G1
Fordyce 41 E2
Forhill 56 D5
Formby 22 B4
Formby 58 A2
Forres 40 B3
Forsbrook 18 C2
Fort Augustus (Cille
  Chuimein) 39 G5
Fort William
  (An Gearasdan) 35 G1
Forth 32 B3
Fortingall 36 B2
Fortis Green 54 D3
Forton 22 C2
Fortrose
  (A' Chananaich) 40 A3
Fortuneswell 6 B6
Forty Green 54 A2
Forty Hill 55 E2
Foster Street 55 F1
Foulden 33 G3
Foulridge 23 E2
Four Ashes (Coven) 56 C2
Four Ashes (Kinver) 56 B4
Four Crosses 56 C2
Four Lane Ends 58 D6
Four Marks 7 G3
**Four Oaks
  (Meriden) 57 F4**
**Four Oaks (Sutton
  Coldfield) 57 E3**
Four Oaks Park 57 E3
Fowey 4 B6
Fowlis Wester 36 C3
Fowlmere 14 C2
Fownhope 12 B3
Fox Hatch 55 G2
Foxhole 3 H4
Foxton 14 C2
Foxwist Green 59 E6
Foyers (Foithir) 39 G4
Fradley 57 E1
Framfield 8 C4
Framlingham 15 G1
Frampton 20 B3
Frampton Cotterell 12 B5
Frampton on Severn 12 C4
Franche 56 B5
Frandley 59 E5
Frankby 58 A4
Frankley 56 C4
Frankton 57 H5
Frant 8 D4
Fraserburgh 41 G2
Freasley 57 F3
Freckleton 22 C3
Freeland 13 F4
Freiston 20 B2
Fremington 4 D2
Freshfield 58 A2
Freshwater 7 F5
Freuchie 36 D4
Friern Barnet 54 D2
Frimley 7 H2
Frinton-on-Sea 15 G4
Friockheim 37 F2
Friskney 20 B2
Frithelstock Stone 4 C3
Frizington 27 F5
Frodsham 22 D6

Frodsham 58 D5
Frog Pool 56 A6
Frogmore *Hants.* 7 H2
Frogmore *Herts.* 54 C1
Frome 6 C2
Fryerning 55 H1
Fulbourn 14 D2
Fulford 18 C3
Fulham 54 D4
Fulmer 54 B3
Furnace 31 E1
Furnace End 57 F3
Fyfield 55 G1
Fyvie 41 F4

G

Gadebridge 54 B1
Gailey 56 C1
Gainford 28 D5
Gainsborough 24 D5
Gairloch (Geàrrloch) 38 D2
Galashiels 32 D4
Gale 59 H1
Galgate 22 C2
Galley Common 57 G3
Galleywood 15 F6
Gallowstree Elm 56 B4
Galston 31 H5
Gamlingay 14 B2
Ganwick Corner 54 D2
Garden City 58 B6
Gardenstown 41 F2
Garelochhead 31 F2
Garforth 24 B3
Gargrave 23 F2
Garmond 41 F3
Garmouth 40 D2
Garrett's Green 57 E4
Garsington 13 G4
Garstang 22 C2
Garston 58 C4
Garswood 58 D3
Garve (Clachan Ghairbh)
  39 G2
Gateacre 58 C4
Gatehouse of Fleet 26 D3
Gateshead 28 D2
Gatesheath 58 C6
Gateside 36 D4
Gathurst 58 D2
Gatley 23 E5
Gatley 59 G4
Gawsworth 59 G5
Gayton *Mersey.* 58 A4
Gayton *Norf.* 20 D4
Geddington 19 G5
Gedney 20 B3
Gee Cross 59 H3
Geirinis 44 B7
Gentleshaw 56 D1
George Green 54 B3
Georgeham 4 C2
Gerrans 3 G5
Gerrards Cross 14 A5
Gerrards Cross 54 B3
Gidea Park 55 G3
Gilberdyke 24 D3
Gillingham *Dorset* 6 C3
Gillingham *Med.* 15 E6
Gills 43 H2
Gilson 57 E3
Gilwern 11 H4
Gin Pit 59 E2
Ginclough 59 H5
Girton 14 C1
Girvan 26 B1
Givons Grove 54 C6
Glamis 37 E2
Glanaman 11 E4
Glascote 57 F2
Glasgow (Glaschu) 31 H3
Glastonbury 6 B3
Glazebrook 59 E3
Glazebury 22 D5
Glazebury 59 E3
Glazeley 58 A4
Gleadsmoss 59 G6
Glemsford 15 E2
Glenbervie 41 F6

Glencaple 27 F2
Glencarse 36 D3
Glencoe
  (A' Chàrnaich) 35 G2
Glenelg (Gleann Eilg)
  38 D5
Glenfarg 36 D4
Glenfinnan (Gleann
  Fhionnainn) 39 E6
Glenkindie 40 D5
Glenmavis 32 A2
Glenridding 27 H5
Glenrothes 36 D4
Glentrool 26 C2
Glinton 20 A3
Glossop 23 F5
Gloucester 12 C4
Glusburn 23 F2
Glynceiriog 17 F4
Glyncoch 11 G5
Glyncorrwg 11 F5
**Glynneath
  (Glyn-Nedd) 11 F4**
Gnosall 18 B3
Gobowen 17 G4
Godalming 8 A3
Godden Green 55 G6
Goddington 55 F5
Godmanchester 14 B1
Godshill 7 G5
Godstone 8 C3
Godstone 55 E6
Goff's Oak 55 E1
Golborne 22 D5
Golborne 59 E3
Golders Green 54 D3
Goldthorn Park 56 C3
Goldthorpe 24 B4
Golspie 40 A1
Goodmayes 55 F3
Goodwick (Wdig) 10 B3
Goodyers End 57 G4
Goole 24 C4
**Goose Green
  Gt.Man. 58 D2**
Goose Green *Kent* 55 H6
Goosehill Green 56 C6
Goosnargh 22 D3
Goostrey 23 E6
Goostrey 59 F5
Gorcott Hill 56 D6
Gordon 33 E3
Gorebridge 32 D2
Gorey 5 H6
Goring 13 G4
Gornalwood 56 C3
Gorran Haven 3 H4
Gorseinon 11 E5
Gorstage 59 E5
Gorton 59 G3
Gosberton 20 A3
Gosfield 15 E3
Gosforth *Cumb.* 27 F5
Gosforth *T. & W.* 28 D2
Gospel End 56 C3
Gosport 7 G5
Gotham 19 F3
Goudhurst 9 E4
Gourdon 37 G1
Gourock 31 F3
Goxhill 25 F3
Grabhair 44 E4
Gradbach 59 H6
Grain 15 E6
Grains Bar 59 H2
Grandborough 57 H6
Grandtully 36 C2
Grange 58 A4
Grange Hill 55 F2
Grange-over-Sands 22 C1
Grangemouth 32 B1
Grantham 19 H3
Grantown-on-Spey 40 B4
Grappenhall 59 E4
Grasmere 27 H5
Grasscroft 23 F4
Grasscroft 59 H2
Grassendale 58 B4
Grassington 23 F1
Grassmoor 24 B6

Gravel Hill 54 B2
Gravelly Hill 57 E3
Gravesend 14 D6
Gravesend 55 H4
Grays 55 H4
Grays 14 D6
Grayshott 7 H3
Greasby 22 B5
Greasby 58 A4
Great Altcar 58 B2
Great Amwell 14 C4
Great Ayton 29 F5
Great Bardfield 14 D3
Great Barford 14 B2
Great Barr 56 D3
Great Barrow 58 C6
Great Barton 15 E1
Great Bentley 15 F3
Great Bookham 8 B3
Great Bookham 54 C6
Great Buckland 55 H5
Great Budworth 59 E5
Great Burstead 55 H2
Great Chatwell 56 A1
Great Chesterford 14 D2
Great Clifton 27 F4
Great Crosby 58 B2
Great Doddington 13 H1
Great Dunmow 14 D3
Great Eccleston 22 C2
Great Ellingham 21 E5
Great Gaddesden 14 A4
Great Glen 19 F5
Great Gonerby 19 G3
Great Harwood 23 E3
Great Haywood 18 C3
Great Heath 57 G4
Great Horkesley 15 F3
Great Houghton 24 B4
Great Kingshill 13 H5
Great Lumley 28 D3
Great Malvern 12 C2
Great Massingham 20 D3
Great Missenden 13 H4
Great Notley 15 E3
Great Oxney Green 55 H1
Great Parndon 55 F1
Great Plumstead 21 G4
Great Preston 24 B3
Great Sankey 58 D4
Great Saredon 56 C2
Great Shelford 14 C2
Great Sutton 58 B5
Great Torrington 4 C3
Great Totham (North)
  Essex 15 E4
Great Totham (South)
  Essex 15 E4
Great Wakering 15 F5
Great Waldingfield 15 F2
Great Waltham 14 D4
Great Warley 55 G2
Great Witley 56 A6
Great Wyrley 18 C4
Great Wyrley 56 C2
Great Yarmouth 21 H4
Great Yeldham 15 E3
Greatham 29 E4
Greatness 55 G6
Green End 57 F4
Green Lane 56 D6
Green Street 54 C2
**Green Street Green
  Gt.Lon. 55 F5**
**Green Street Green
  Kent 55 G4**
Greenfield
  (Maes-Glas) 22 B6
Greenford 54 C3
Greenham 13 F6
Greenheys 59 F2
Greenhill 54 C3
Greenhithe 55 G4
Greenlooming 36 B4
Greenmount 59 F1
Greenock 31 F3
Greens Norton 13 G2
Greensted 55 G1
Greensted Green 55 G1

Greenwich 55 E4
Greetland 23 F3
Grendon 57 F3
Grendon Common 57 F3
Grendon Underwood 13 G4
Gresford 17 G3
Gress (Griais) 44 E2
Gretna 27 H2
Gretton 12 D3
Griff 57 G4
Grimeford Village 59 E1
Grimley 56 B6
Grimsargh 22 D3
Grimsby 25 F4
Grimshader (Griomsadar)
   44 E3
Grimston 20 D3
Grindle 56 A2
Groby 19 F4
Grove 13 F5
Grove Park 55 F4
Grovehill 54 B1
Grundisburgh 15 G2
Guardbridge 37 E4
Guide Post 28 D1
Guilden Sutton 58 C6
Guildford 8 A3
Guildtown 36 D3
Guisborough 29 F5
Guiseley 24 A2
Gullane 32 D1
Gunnersbury 54 C4
Gunness 24 D4
Gunnislake 4 C5
Gunstone 56 B2
Gurnett 59 H5
Gurnos 11 F4
Guthrie 37 F2
Gwauncaegurwen 11 F4
Gwernaffield 58 A6
Gwernymynydd 58 A6
Gwersyllt 17 G3

H

Habost (Tabost) 44 F1
Hackbridge 54 D5
Hackleton 13 H2
Hackney 55 E3
Hacton 55 G3
Haddenham Bucks. 13 H4
Haddenham Cambs. 14 C1
Haddington 33 E2
Hademore 57 E2
Hadfield 23 F5
Hadleigh Essex 15 E5
Hadleigh Suff. 15 F2
Hadley 56 B6
Hadley Wood 54 D2
Hadlow 8 D3
Hadston 28 D1
Hadzor 56 C6
Haggerston 55 E3
Hagley 18 C5
Hagley 56 C4
Hague Bar 59 H4
Haigh 59 E2
Hailey 13 F4
Hailsham 8 D5
Hainault 55 F2
Halberton 5 F3
Hale Gt.Man. 23 E5
Hale Gt.Man. 59 F4
Hale Halton 22 C5
Hale Halton 58 C4
Hale Bank 58 C4
Hale Barns 59 F4
Halesowen 18 C5
Halesowen 56 C4
Halesworth 15 H1
Halewood 56 C4
Halfpenny Green 56 B3
Halifax 23 F3
Halkirk 43 G3
Halkyn 58 A5
Hall Green 57 E4
Halling 14 D6
Halliwell 59 E1
Hallow 12 C2
Halls Green 55 F1

Halsall 58 B1
Halstead Essex 15 E3
Halstead Kent 55 F5
Halton Bucks. 13 H4
Halton Halton 58 D4
Halton Lancs. 22 D1
Haltwhistle 28 B2
Ham 54 C4
Ham Green 56 D6
Ham Hill 55 H5
Hamble-le-Rice 7 F4
Hambleton Lancs. 22 C2
Hambleton N.Yorks. 24 C3
Hamilton 32 A3
Hammersmith 54 D4
Hammerwich 18 C4
Hammerwich 56 D2
Hammond Street 55 E1
Hampstead 54 D4
Hampton Gt.Lon. 54 C5
Hampton Shrop. 56 A4
Hampton Loade 56 A4
Hampton Lovett 56 B6
Hampton Wick 54 C5
Hampton in Arden 57 F4
Hampton on the
   Hill 57 F6
Hamstall Ridware 57 E1
Hamstreet 9 F4
Hanbury 56 C6
Handbridge 58 C6
Handforth 59 G4
Handley Green 55 H1
Handsacre 18 C4
Handsacre 56 D1
Handsworth 56 D3
Hanley Castle 12 C2
Hanslope 13 H2
Hanthorpe 19 H3
Hanwell 54 C4
Hanwood 17 G5
Hanworth 54 C4
Hapsford 58 C5
Hapton 23 E3
Harborne 56 D4
Harborough Magna 57 H5
Harbury 13 F2
Harden 23 F3
Harden 56 D2
Hardingstone 13 H2
Hardwick 17 C2
Hardwick 56 D3
Hardwicke 12 C4
Harefield 54 B2
Hargrave 58 C6
Harlaston 57 F1
Harlesden 54 D3
Harleston 21 F5
Harlington
   Cen.Beds. 14 A3
Harlington Gt.Lon. 54 B4
Harlow 14 C4
Harmondsworth 54 B4
Harold Hill 55 G2
Harold Park 55 G2
Harold Wood 55 G2
Haroldswick 45 J1
Harpenden 14 B4
Harpole 13 G1
Harpurhey 59 G2
Harrietfield 36 C3
Harrietsham 9 E3
Harringay 55 E3
Harrogate 23 B2
Harrold 14 A2
Harrow 54 C3
Harrow Weald 54 C2
Harrow on the Hill 54 C3
Harston 14 C2
Hartfield 8 C4
Hartford 22 D6
Hartford 59 E5
Harthill 32 B2
Hartland 4 B2
Hartlebury 12 C1
Hartlebury 56 B5

Hartlepool 29 F4
Hartley 14 D6
Hartley 55 H5
Hartley Wintney 7 H2
Hartshill 19 E5
Hartshill 57 G3
Hartshorne 19 E3
Hartwell 13 H2
Harvel 55 H5
Harvington 12 D2
Harvington
   (Kidderminster) 56 B5
Harwell 13 F5
Harwich 15 G3
Harwood 59 F1
Harworth 24 C5
Hasbury 56 C4
Haseley 57 F6
Haseley Knob 57 F5
Haskayne 58 B2
Haslemere 8 A4
Haslingden 23 E3
Haslingfield 14 C2
Haslington 18 B2
Hastings 9 E5
Hastingwood 55 F1
Hastoe 54 A1
Haswell 29 E3
Hatch End 54 C2
Hatchmere 58 D5
Hatfield Herts. 14 B4
Hatfield S.Yorks. 24 C4
Hatfield Broad Oak 14 D4
Hatfield Heath 14 D4
Hatfield Peverel 15 E4
Hatherleigh 4 D3
Hathern 19 F3
Hathersage 24 B5
Hathershaw 59 H2
Hatherton 56 D5
Hatton Aber. 41 G4
Hatton Derbys. 18 D3
Hatton Gt.Lon. 54 C4
Hatton Warr. 58 D4
Hatton Warks. 57 F6
Hatton Heath 58 C6
Hatton of Fintray 41 F5
Haughley 15 F1
Haughton 18 B3
Haughton Green 59 H3
Haunton 57 F1
Havannah 59 G6
Havant 7 H4
Haverfordwest
   (Hwlffordd) 10 B4
Haverhill 14 D2
Havering Park 55 F2
Havering-atte-Bower
   55 G2
Hawarden
   (Penarlâg) 22 C6
Hawarden
   (Penarlâg) 58 B6
Hawes 28 B6
Hawick 33 E5
Hawkes End 57 F4
Hawkhurst 9 E4
Hawkinge 9 E3
Hawkshead 27 H6
Hawkwell 15 E5
Hawley 55 G4
Hawley's Corner 55 F6
Haworth 23 F3
Haxby 24 C2
Haxey 24 D5
Hay Mills 57 E4
Hay-on-Wye (Y Gelli
   Gandryll) 11 H2
Haydock 22 D5
Haydock 56 D3
Haydon Bridge 28 B2
Hayes (Bromley) 55 F5
Hayes (Hillingdon) 54 B3
Hayes End 54 B3
Hayfield 23 F5
Hayle 3 F5
Haywards Heath 8 C4
Hazel Grove 23 F5
Hazel Grove 59 H4

Hazelhurst 59 F1
Hazelslade 56 D1
Hazelwood 55 F5
Hazlemere 13 H5
Heacham 20 C3
Headbourne Worthy 7 F3
Headcorn 9 E3
Headless Cross 56 D6
Headley Hants. 7 H3
Headley Surr. 54 D6
Headley Heath 56 D5
Heady Hill 59 G1
Heage 19 E2
Heald Green 59 G4
Healey 59 G1
Healing 25 F4
Heanor 19 E2
Heap Bridge 59 G1
Heath Hayes 56 D1
Heath Hill 56 A1
Heath Town 56 C3
Heath and Reach 14 A3
Heather 57 G1
Heathfield Devon 5 E5
Heathfield E.Suss. 8 D4
Heathrow Airport 54 B4
Heathton 56 B3
Heatley 59 F4
Heaton 59 H6
Heaton Moor 59 G3
Heaton's Bridge 58 C1
Heaverham 55 G6
Heaviley 59 H4
Hebden Bridge 23 F3
Hebden Green 59 E6
Heckington 20 A2
Heckmondwike 24 A3
Heddon-on-the-Wall
   28 D2
Hedge End 7 F4
Hedgerley 54 A3
Hednesford 18 C4
Hednesford 56 D1
Hedon 25 F3
Hedsor 54 A3
Heighington Darl. 28 D4
Heighington Lincs. 25 E6
Heightington 56 A5
Helensburgh 31 F2
Hellister 45 H4
Helmsdale 43 F5
Helmsley 29 F6
Helsby 22 D6
Helsby 58 C5
Helston 3 F5
Hemel Hempstead 14 A4
Hemingford Grey 14 B1
Hempnall 21 F5
Hemsby 21 G4
Hemsworth 24 B4
Hemyock 5 G3
Henbury 59 G5
Hendon 54 D3
Henfield 8 B5
Henham 14 D3
Henley Park 54 A6
Henley-in-Arden 13 E1
Henley-in-Arden 57 E6
Henley-on-Thames 13 H5
Henlow 14 B3
Henstridge 6 C4
Hereford 12 B2
Hermitage 13 G6
Hermitage Green 59 E3
Herne Bay 15 G6
Herne Pound 55 H6
Herongate 55 H2
Heronsgate 54 B2
Hersham 54 C5
Herstmonceux 8 D5
Hertford 14 C4
Heskin Green 58 D1
Hessle 25 E3
Heston 54 C4
Heswall 22 B5
Heswall 58 A4
Hethersett 21 F4
Hetton-le-Hole 29 E3
Hewell Grange 56 D6

Hewell Lane 56 D6
Hexham 28 C2
Hextable 14 D6
Hextable 55 G4
Heybridge (Ingatestone)
   55 H2
Heysham 22 C1
Heyside 59 H2
Heywood 23 E4
Heywood 59 G1
Hibaldstow 25 E4
High Beach 55 F2
High Bentham 22 D1
High Crompton 59 H2
High Etherley 28 D4
High Halden 9 E4
High Halstow 15 E6
High Heath 56 D2
High Lane 23 F5
High Lane 59 H4
High Laver 55 G1
High Legh 23 E5
High Legh 59 F4
High Littleton 6 B3
High Lorton 27 G4
High Ongar 14 D4
High Ongar 55 G1
High Onn 56 B1
High Town 56 C1
High Wycombe 13 H5
Higham Derbys. 19 E2
Higham Kent 15 E6
Higham Ferrers 14 A1
Higham on the Hill
   57 G3
Highampton 4 C3
Highams Park 55 E2
Highbridge 6 A2
Highclere 13 F6
Higher Blackley 59 G2
Higher Folds 22 D4
Higher Folds 59 E2
Higher Green 59 F3
Higher Kinnerton 58 B6
Higher Walton
   Lancs. 22 D3
Higher Walton
   Warr. 58 D4
Higher Whitley 59 E4
Higher Wincham 59 E5
Higher Woodhill 59 F1
Highfields 14 C2
Highgate 54 D3
Highlane 59 G6
Highley 18 B5
Highley 56 A4
Highnam 12 C4
Highter's Heath 56 D5
Hightown 22 C4
Hightown 58 A2
Highwood Hill 54 D2
Highworth 13 E5
Hildenborough 8 D3
Hilgay 20 C5
Hill 57 H6
Hill End 54 B2
Hill Ridware 56 D1
Hill Wootton 57 G6
Hill of Fearn 40 A2
Hilliard's Cross 57 E1
Hillingdon 54 B3
Hillside Angus 37 G1
Hillside Worcs. 56 A6
Hillswick 45 G3
Hilperton 6 C2
Hilton Derbys. 18 D3
Hilton Shrop. 56 A3
Hilton Staffs. 56 D2
Hilton of Cadboll 40 A2
Himley 56 B3
Hinchley Wood 54 C5
Hinckley 19 E5
Hinckley 57 H3
Hinderton 58 B5
Hindhead 7 H3
Hindley 23 E4
Hindley 59 E2
Hindley Green 59 E2
Hingham 21 E4
Hinksford 56 B4

Hinton 13 G2
Hints 57 E2
Hirwaun 11 G4
Histon 14 C1
Hitcham 54 A3
Hitchin 14 B3
Hither Green 55 E4
Hixon 18 C3
Hobbs Cross 55 F2
Hockley 15 E5
Hockley Heath 13 E1
Hockley Heath 57 E5
Hockwold cum
  Wilton 20 D5
Hoddesdon 14 C4
Hoddesdon 55 E1
Hodgehill 59 G6
Hodnet 18 A3
Hodsoll Street 55 H5
Hoggrill's End 57 F3
Holbeach 20 B3
Holbrook 15 G3
Holbrooks 57 G4
Holbury 7 F4
Holcombe 59 F1
Holders Hill 54 D3
Holland 55 E2
Hollingworth 23 F5
Hollins Green 59 E3
Hollinwood 59 H2
Hollywood 56 D5
Holme 22 D1
Holme-on-Spalding-Moor
  24 D3
Holmer Green 54 A2
Holmes 58 C1
Holmes Chapel 23 E6
Holmes Chapel 59 F6
Holmesfield 24 B6
Holmeswood 58 C1
Holmfirth 24 A4
Holmsgarth 45 H4
Holsworthy 4 C3
Holt Norf. 21 E3
Holt Wilts. 12 C6
Holt Worcs. 56 B6
Holt End 13 E6
Holt End 56 D6
Holt Fleet 56 B6
Holt Heath 56 B6
Holton le Clay 25 F4
Holtspur 54 A3
Holy Cross 56 C5
Holyfield 55 E1
Holyhead
  (Caergybi) 16 A1
Holytown 32 A2
Holywell
  (Treffynnon) 22 B6
Holywell Green 23 F4
Honeybourne 13 E2
Honiley 57 F5
Honiton 5 G3
Honley 24 A4
Hoo Green 59 F4
Hoo St Werburgh 15 E6
Hook E.Riding 24 D3
Hook Gt.Lon. 54 C5
Hook Hants. 7 H2
Hook Green 55 G4
Hook Green
  (Meopham) 55 H5
Hook Green
  (Southfleet) 55 H4
Hook Norton 13 F3
Hoole 58 C6
Hooley 54 D6
Hooton 58 B5
Hope 17 G3
Hopeman 40 C2
Hopsford 57 H4
Hopstone 56 A3
Hopton 21 H4
Hopwas 57 E2
Hopwood 56 D5
Horam 8 D5
Horbury 24 A4
Horden 29 E3
Hordle 7 E5
Horley 8 B3

Horn Hill 54 B2
Horncastle 25 F6
Hornchurch 55 G3
Horndean 7 H4
Horndon on the
  Hill 55 H3
Horning 21 G4
Horns Green 55 F6
Hornsea 25 F2
Hornsey 55 E3
Horrabridge 4 D5
Horringer 15 E1
Horrocks Fold 59 F1
Horsebrook 56 B1
Horsell 54 A6
Horsford 21 F4
Horsforth 24 A3
Horsham 8 A3
Horsmonden 9 E3
Horspath 13 G4
Horsted Keynes 8 C4
Horton 54 B4
Horton Heath 7 F4
Horton Kirby 55 G5
Horwich 22 D4
Horwich 59 E1
Hoscar 58 C1
Hough Green 58 C4
Houghton 14 B1
Houghton Conquest 14 A2
Houghton le Spring 29 E3
Hounslow 14 B6
Hounslow 54 C4
Houston 31 G3
Houton 45 C3
Hove 8 B5
Hoveton 21 G4
Howden 24 D3
Howwood 31 G3
Hoylake 22 B5
Hoylake 58 A4
Hoyland 24 B4
Hucknall 19 F2
Huddersfield 24 A4
Huddlesford 57 E2
Hugglescote 57 H1
Hugh Town 3 F3
Hughenden Valley 14 H5
Huish Episcopi 6 A3
Hullavington 12 C5
Hullbridge 15 E5
Hulme Walfield 59 G6
Hundleton 10 B4
Hundon 15 E2
Hungerford 13 F6
Hunmanby 25 F1
Hunningham 57 G6
Hunningham Hill 57 G6
Hunstanton 20 C2
Hunt End 56 D6
Hunt's Cross 58 C4
Huntingdon 14 A1
Huntington 56 C1
Huntly 41 E3
Hunton Bridge 54 B1
Hurdsfield 59 H5
Hurley 13 H5
Hurley 57 F3
Hurlford 31 G5
Hurlston Green 58 B1
Hurst Green E.Suss. 9 E4
Hurst Green Surr. 55 E6
Hurstpierpoint 8 B5
Hurworth-on-Tees 29 E5
Hutton Essex 55 H2
Hutton Lancs. 22 C3
Hutton N.Som. 6 A2
Hutton Cranswick 25 E2
Hutton Mount 55 H2
Hutton Rudby 29 E5
Huxley 58 D6
Huyton 22 C5
Huyton 58 C3
Hyde 23 F5
Hyde 59 H3
Hyde Heath 54 A1
Hyde Lea 56 C1
Hythe Hants. 7 F4
Hythe Kent 9 G4
Hythe End 54 B4

I

Ibstock 19 E4
Ibstock 57 H1
Ickenham 54 B3
Ickford 13 H3
Icklesham 9 E5
Ide Hill 55 F6
Ightham 55 G6
Ilchester 6 B3
Ilford 14 C5
Ilford 55 F3
Ilfracombe 4 D1
Ilkeston 19 E2
Ilkley 24 A2
Illey 56 C4
Illidge Green 59 F6
Ilminster 6 A4
Immingham 25 F4
Impington 14 C1
Ince 58 C5
Ince Blundell 58 B2
Ince-in-Makerfield 22 D4
Ince-in-Makerfield 58 D2
Inchture 36 D3
Ingatestone 14 D5
Ingatestone 55 H2
Ingleton 22 D1
Ingoldmells 25 H6
Ingrave 55 H2
Inkberrow 12 D2
Innellan 31 F3
Innerleithen 32 D4
Insch 41 E4
Insh 40 A5
Inver 40 A1
Inveralligin 38 D3
Inverallochy 41 G2
Inveraray
  (Inbhir Aora) 31 E1
Inverbervie 37 G1
Invergarry
  (Inbhir Garadh) 39 F5
Invergordon 40 A2
Inverie 38 D6
Inverkeilor 37 F2
Inverkeithing 32 C1
Inverkeithny 41 E3
Inverkip 31 F3
Invermoriston (Inbhir
  Moireasdan) 39 G5
Inverness
  (Inbhir Nis) 39 H3
Inverurie 41 F4
Ipplepen 5 E5
Ipstones 18 C2
Ipswich 15 G2
Irby 58 A4
Irby Hill 58 A4
Irchester 14 A1
Irlam 23 E5
Irlam 59 F3
Iron Acton 12 B5
Ironbridge 18 A4
Irthlingborough 14 A1
Irvine 31 G5
Isleham 14 D1
Isleornsay
  (Eilean Iarmain) 38 C5
Isleworth 54 C4
Istead Rise 14 D6
Istead Rise 55 H5
Iver 14 A5
Iver 54 B3
Iver Heath 14 A5
Iver Heath 54 B3
Ivetsey Bank 56 B1
Ivy Hatch 55 G6
Ivybridge 4 D6
Iwade 15 F6
Ixworth 15 F1

J

Jacksdale 19 E2
Jacobswell 54 A6
Jamestown 31 G2
Jarrow 29 E2
Jaywick 15 G4
Jedburgh 33 E4

Jericho 59 G1
Jodrell Bank 59 F5
John o'Groats 43 H2
Johnshaven 37 G1
Johnston 10 B4
Johnstone 31 G3
Johnstonebridge 27 F1
Jordans 54 A2

K

Keadby 24 D4
Kearsley 59 F2
Keckwick 58 D4
Kedington 15 E2
Keelby 25 F4
Keele 18 B2
Kegworth 19 E3
Keig 41 E5
Keighley 23 F2
Keiss 43 H2
Keith 40 D3
Kelsall 22 D6
Kelsall 58 D6
Kelso 33 F4
Kelty 32 C1
Kelvedon 15 E4
Kelvedon Hatch 14 D5
Kelvedon Hatch 55 G2
Kemberton 56 A2
Kemnay 41 F5
Kemps Green 57 E5
Kempsey 12 C2
Kempsford 13 E5
Kempston 14 A2
Kemsing 41 F3
Kemsing 55 G6
Kemsley 15 F6
Kendal 28 A6
Kenilworth 13 E1
Kenilworth 57 F5
Kenley 55 E5
Kenmore 36 B2
Kennacraig 30 D3
Kennethmont 41 E4
Kennoway 37 E4
Kensington 54 D3
Kent Street 55 H6
Kentish Town 54 D3
Kenton 5 F4
Kenwyn 4 C3
Kenyon 59 E3
Keresley 57 G4
Kerridge 59 H5
Kessingland 21 H5
Keston 55 F5
Keswick 27 G4
Kettering 13 H1
Kettlebrook 57 F2
Kettleshulme 59 H5
Ketton 19 H4
Kevingtown 55 F5
Kew 54 C4
Kewstoke 12 A6
Kexbrough 24 B4
Key Green 59 G6
Keyingham 25 F3
Keymer 8 C5
Keynsham 12 B6
Keyworth 19 F3
Kibworth Beauchamp 19 F5
Kibworth Harcourt 19 F5
Kidbrooke 55 F5
Kiddemore Green 56 B2
Kidderminster 13 F1
Kidderminster 56 B5
Kidlington 13 F4
Kidmore End 13 G6
Kidsgrove 18 B2
Kidwelly (Cydweli) 10 D4
Kilbarchan 31 G3
Kilberry 30 D3
Kilbirnie 31 G4
Kilburn Derbys. 19 E2
Kilburn Gt.Lon. 54 D3
Kilchoan 34 C1
Kilchrenan
  (Cill Chrèanain) 35 F3
Kilcreggan 31 F2

Killamarsh 24 B5
Killearn 31 H2
Killin 36 A3
Killinghall 24 A2
Killmacolm 31 G3
Kilmany 37 E3
Kilmarnock 31 G5
Kilmartin 30 D2
Kilmaurs 31 G4
Kilmelford 30 D1
Kilmorack 39 G3
Kilrenny 37 F4
Kilsby 13 G1
Kilsyth 32 A2
Kiltarlity 39 H3
Kilwinning 31 G4
Kimberley 19 F2
Kimpton 14 B4
Kinbrace 43 E4
Kinbuck 36 B4
Kincardine 32 B1
Kincardine O'Neil 41 E6
Kincraig 40 A5
Kindallachan 36 C2
Kineton 13 F2
Kineton Green 57 E4
King's Bromley 57 E1
King's Heath 56 D4
King's Hill W.Mid. 56 C3
King's Hill Warks. 57 G5
King's Lynn 20 C3
King's Moss 58 D2
King's Newnham 57 H5
King's Nympton 5 E3
King's Somborne 7 F3
King's Sutton 13 G3
Kinghorn 32 C1
Kings Hill 8 D3
Kings Hill 55 H6
Kings Langley 14 A4
Kings Langley 54 B1
Kings Worthy 7 F3
Kingsbarns 37 F4
Kingsbridge 5 E6
Kingsbury Gt.Lon. 54 C3
Kingsbury Warks. 18 D5
Kingsbury Warks. 57 F3
Kingsbury Episcopi 6 A3
Kingsclere 7 G2
Kingsdown 9 H3
Kingsford 56 B4
Kingshurst 57 E4
Kingskerswell 5 E5
Kingsley
  Ches.W. & C. 22 D6
Kingsley
  Ches.W. & C. 58 D5
Kingsley Staffs. 18 C2
Kingslow 56 A3
Kingsmoor 55 F1
Kingsnorth 9 F4
Kingstanding 56 D3
Kingsteignton 5 E5
Kingston Gt.Man. 59 H3
Kingston Moray 40 D2
Kingston Bagpuize 13 F5
Kingston upon Hull 25 F3
Kingston upon
  Thames 14 B6
Kingston upon
  Thames 54 C5
Kingstone 12 A3
Kingswear 5 E6
Kingswells 41 F5
Kingswinford 56 B4
Kingswood Glos. 12 C5
Kingswood S.Glos. 12 B6
Kingswood Surr. 54 D6
Kingswood Warks. 57 E5
Kington 11 H2
Kingussie 40 A5
Kinlet 56 A4
Kinloch High. 38 B6
Kinloch P. & K. 36 D2
Kinloch Rannoch 36 A2
Kinlochbervie 42 B3
Kinlochewe 37 F3
Kinlochleven (Ceann Loch
  Liobhann) 35 G1

Kinlochmore 35 G1
Kinloss 40 B2
Kinmel Bay
   (Bae Cinmel) 22 A5
Kinnaird 36 D3
Kinnerton Green 58 B6
Kinross 36 D4
Kinrossie 36 D3
Kintbury 13 F6
Kintore 41 F5
Kinver 18 B5
Kinver 56 B4
Kippax 24 B3
Kippington 55 G6
Kirby Corner 57 F5
Kirby Muxloe 19 F4
Kirk Ella 25 E3
Kirkbean 27 F3
Kirkbride 28 D6
Kirkburton 24 A4
Kirkby 22 C5
Kirkby 58 C3
Kirkby Lonsdale 22 D1
Kirkby Mallory 57 H2
Kirkby Stephen 28 B5
Kirkby in Ashfield 19 E2
Kirkbymoorside 29 F6
Kirkcaldy 32 C1
Kirkcolm 26 A2
Kirkconnel 32 A5
Kirkcudbright 26 D3
Kirkham 22 C3
Kirkhill 39 H3
Kirkintilloch 31 H3
Kirkliston 32 C2
Kirkmichael 36 C1
Kirkmuirhill 32 A3
Kirkton of Glenisla 36 D1
Kirkton of
   Kingoldrum 37 E2
Kirkton of Maryculter 41 F6
Kirkton of Rayne 41 E4
Kirkton of Skene 41 F5
Kirktown of Alvah 41 E2
Kirktown of Deskford 41 E2
Kirkwall 45 C3
Kirriemuir 37 E2
Kirtomy 43 E2
Kirton *Lincs.* 20 B3
Kirton *Suff.* 15 G3
Kirton in Lindsey 25 E5
Kislingbury 13 G2
Kites Hardwick 57 H6
Kitt's End 54 D2
Kitt's Green 57 E4
Knaphill 54 A6
Knaresborough 24 B2
Knebworth 14 B4
Knighton
   (Tref-y-clawdd) 11 H1
Knockandhu 40 C4
Knockholt 55 F6
Knockholt Pound 55 F6
Knockmill 55 G5
Knolls Green 59 G5
Knott End-on-Sea 22 C2
Knottingley 24 C3
Knotty Green 54 A2
Knowle 13 E1
Knowle 57 E5
Knowsley 22 C5
Knowsley 58 C3
Knutsford 23 E6
Knutsford 59 F5
Kyle of Lochalsh (Caol Loch
   Aillse) 38 D4
Kyleakin (Caol Acain) 38 D4

L

Laceby 25 F4
Lacey Green 13 H4
Lach Dennis 59 F5
Lacock 12 D6
Ladywood 56 B6
Laggan 39 H6
Laide 38 D1
Laindon 55 H3
Lairg 42 D5

Lakenheath 20 D5
Lakeside 55 G4
Laleham 54 B5
Laleston 11 F6
Lamberhurst 8 D4
Lambourn 13 F6
Lambourne End 55 F2
Lamington 40 A2
Lamlash 31 E5
Lampeter (Llanbedr Pont
   Steffan) 11 E2
Lanark 32 A3
Lancaster 22 C1
Lanchester 28 D3
Lancing 8 B5
Landford 7 E4
Landican 58 A4
Landkey 4 D2
Landywood 56 C2
Lane End *Bucks.* 13 H5
Lane End *Kent* 55 G4
Lane Ends 59 H3
Lane Green 56 B2
Lane Head 59 E3
Lanesfield 56 C3
Langdon Hills 55 H3
Langford 14 B2
Langham 19 G4
Langho 22 D3
Langholm 27 H1
Langley *Ches.E.* 59 H5
Langley *Gt.Man.* 59 H3
Langley *Slo.* 54 B4
Langley *Warks.* 56 D6
Langley Corner 54 B3
Langley Green 57 F6
Langley Mill 19 E2
Langley Park 28 D3
Langold 24 C5
Langport 6 A3
Langstone *Hants.* 7 H4
Langstone *Newport* 12 A5
Langtoft 20 A4
Lanivet 3 H3
Lapley 56 B1
Lapworth 57 E5
Larbert 32 A1
Largoward 37 E4
Largs 31 F4
Larkhall 32 A3
Larkhill 7 E2
Lasswade 32 D2
Latchford 59 E4
Lately Common 59 E3
Latheron 43 G4
Latheronwheel 43 G4
Latimer 54 B2
Lauder 33 E3
Launceston 4 C4
Launton 13 G3
Laurencekirk 37 G1
Lavenham 15 F2
Law 32 A3
Lawers 36 A3
Lawford 15 F3
Laxey 26 C5
Layer de la Haye 15 F4
Layter's Green 54 A2
Lea Marston 57 F3
Leamington
   Hastings 57 H6
Leamington Spa 57 G6
Leasingham 19 H2
Leasowe 58 A3
Leatherhead 8 B3
Leatherhead 54 C6
Leaves Green 55 F5
Leavesden Green 54 C1
Lechlade-on-Thames 13 E5
Leconfield 25 E2
Ledbury 12 D1
Ledsham 58 B5
Lee Chapel 55 H3
Lee Clump 54 A1
Lee-on-the-Solent 7 G4
Leeds 24 A3
Leek 18 C2
Leek Wootton 57 F6
Leeming 28 D6
Lees 59 H2

Leeswood 22 B6
Leftwich 59 E5
Leicester 19 F4
Leigh 22 D4
Leigh 59 E2
Leighton Buzzard 14 A3
Leiston 15 H1
Lenham 9 E3
Lennoxtown 31 H3
Lent Rise 54 A3
Lenzie 31 H3
Leominster 12 A2
Leonard Stanley 12 C4
Lerwick 45 H2
Leslie 36 D4
Lesmahagow 32 A4
Lessness Heath 55 F4
Letchmore Heath 54 C2
Letchworth Garden
   City 14 B3
Letham *Angus* 37 F2
Letham *Fife* 37 E4
Letterston 10 B3
Leuchars 37 E3
Leumrabhagh 44 E4
Levedale 56 B1
Leven *E.Riding* 25 F2
Leven *Fife* 37 E4
Levens 27 H6
Levenshulme 59 G3
Levenwick 45 H5
Leverburgh (An T-Òb) 44 C5
Leverstock Green 54 B1
Lewes 8 C5
Lewisham 14 C6
Lewisham 55 E4
Lewiston
   (Blàr na Maigh) 39 H4
Leybourne 55 H6
Leyburn 28 D6
Leyland 22 D3
Leysdown-on-Sea 15 F6
Leyton 55 E3
Leytonstone 55 E3
Lhanbryde 40 C2
Lichfield 18 D4
Lichfield 57 E2
Lickey 56 C5
Lickey End 56 C5
Lidlington 14 A3
Lighthorne 13 F2
Lightwater 14 A6
Lightwater 54 A5
Lilleshall 18 B4
Lilleshall 56 A1
Lillington 57 G6
Lilyhurst 56 A1
Lime Side 59 H2
Limefield 59 G1
Limehurst 59 H2
Limpsfield 8 C3
Limpsfield 55 F6
Limpsfield Chart 55 F6
Lincoln 25 E6
Lincomb 56 B6
Lindfield 8 C4
Lindford 7 H3
Lindow End 59 G5
Linfitts 59 H2
Linford 14 D6
Linford 55 H4
Lingdale 29 F5
Lingfield 8 C3
Lingley Green 58 D4
Lingwood 21 G4
Linksness 45 B3
Linlithgow 32 B2
Lintmill 41 E2
Linton *Cambs.* 14 D2
Linton *Derbys.* 18 D5
Linton *Derbys.* 57 F1
Linton-on-Ouse 24 B1
Linwood 31 G3
Liphook 7 H3
Liscard 58 B3
Liskeard 4 B5
Liss 7 H3
Lisvane 11 H5
Litherland 22 C5

Litherland 58 B3
Little Alne 57 E6
Little Altcar 58 B2
Little Amwell 14 C4
Little Aston 56 D3
Little Baddow 15 E4
Little Barrow 58 C6
Little Berkhamsted 54 D1
Little Bloxwich 56 D2
Little Bollington 59 F4
Little Bookham 54 C6
Little Brechin 37 F1
Little Budworth 58 D6
Little Burstead 55 H2
Little Chalfont 54 A2
Little Clacton 15 G4
Little Crosby 58 B2
Little Downham 20 C5
Little Dunkeld 36 C2
Little Eaton 19 E2
Little End 55 G1
Little Gaddesden 14 A4
Little Hay 57 E2
Little Haywood 18 C3
Little Heath 57 G4
Little Hulton 59 F2
Little Laver 55 G1
Little Lawford 57 H5
Little Leigh 59 E5
Little Lever 23 E4
Little Lever 59 F2
Little Missenden 54 A2
Little Neston 58 A5
Little Oakley 15 G3
Little Onn 56 B1
Little Orton 57 G2
Little Packington 57 F4
Little Paxton 14 B1
Little Plumstead 21 G4
Little Stanney 58 C5
Little Sutton 58 B5
Little Thurrock 55 H4
Little Town 59 E3
Little Twycross 57 G2
Little Wakering 15 F5
Little Waltham 15 E4
Little Warley 55 H2
Little Witley 56 B6
Little Woodcote 54 D5
Little Wyrley 56 D2
Littleborough 23 F4
Littleborough 59 H1
Littlebourne 9 G3
Littledean 12 B4
Littlehampton 8 A5
Littlemoss 59 H3
Littleport 20 C5
Littleton
   Ches.W. & C. 58 C6
Littleton *Hants.* 7 F3
Littleton *Surr.* 54 B5
Littleworth 56 D1
Liverpool 22 C5
Liverpool 58 B3
Liverpool John Lennon
   Airport 58 C4
Liversedge 24 A3
Livingston 32 B2
Lizard 3 G6
Llan-non 11 E1
Llanaelhaearn 16 B3
Llanarth 10 D2
Llanbedr 16 C4
Llanbedrog 16 B4
Llanberis 16 C2
Llanbister 11 H1
Llanblethian 11 G6
Llanddowror 10 C4
Llanddulas 22 A6
Llandeilo 11 E3
Llandinam 17 E6
Llandovery
   (Llanymddyfri) 11 F3
Llandrillo 17 E3
Llandrindod Wells 11 G1
Llandudno 16 D1
Llandybie 11 E4
Llandygai 16 C2
Llandysul 10 D2
Llanelli 11 E4

Llanfair Caereinion 17 F5
Llanfairfechan 16 C2
Llanfair Pwllgwyngyll 16 C2
Llanfyllin 17 F5
Llangadfan 17 E5
Llangadog 11 F3
Llangefni 16 B2
Llangeler 10 D3
Llangoed 16 C2
Llangollen 17 F3
Llangrannog 10 D2
Llangurig 11 G1
Llangwm 10 B4
Llanharan 11 G5
Llanharry 11 G5
Llanhilleth 11 H4
Llanidloes 17 E6
Llanilar 11 E1
Llannon 11 E4
Llanrug 16 C2
Llanrwst 16 D2
Llansanffraid Glan
   Conwy 16 D2
Llansannan 22 A6
Llantrisant 11 G5
Llantwit Major 11 G6
Llanuwchllyn 16 D4
Llanwddyn 17 E5
Llanwrda 11 F3
Llanybydder 11 E2
Llay 17 G3
Llong 58 A6
Llwyngwril 16 C5
Llysfaen 16 D2
Loanhead 32 C2
Lochaline
   (Loch Àlainn) 34 D2
Locharbriggs 27 F1
Lochawe (Loch Obha) 35 G3
Lochboisdale (Loch
   Baghasdail) 44 B9
Lochbuie 34 D3
Lochcarron
   (Loch Carrann) 38 D4
Lochdon 35 E3
Lochearnhead (Ceann Loch
   Èireann) 36 A3
Lochgelly 32 C1
Lochgilphead (Ceann Loch
   Gilb) 30 D2
Lochgoilhead 31 F1
Lochinver
   (Loch an Inbhir) 42 A4
Lochmaben 27 F1
Lochmaddy 44 C6
Lochranza 31 E4
Lochwinnoch 31 G4
Lockerbie 27 G1
Locking 6 A2
Locks Heath 7 G4
Locksbottom 55 F5
Loddiswell 5 E6
Loddon 21 G5
Lofthouse 24 B3
Loftus 29 G5
Logan 31 H5
Loggerheads 18 B3
Logie Coldstone 40 D5
Logie Pert 37 F1
Logierait 36 C2
London 14 C5
London 55 E3
London City Airport 55 F3
London Colney 54 C1
London Heathrow
   Airport 54 B4
Long Ashton 12 B6
Long Bank 56 A5
Long Bennington 19 G2
Long Buckby 13 G1
Long Crendon 13 G4
Long Eaton 19 E3
Long Green 58 C5
Long Hanborough 13 F4
Long Itchington 13 F1
Long Itchington 57 H6
Long Lawford 13 F1
Long Lawford 57 H5
Long Melford 15 E2
Long Stratton 21 F5

Long Sutton 20 B3
Longbenton 28 D2
Longbridge *W.Mid.* **56 D5**
Longbridge *Warks.* **57 F6**
Longcross 54 A5
Longdon 56 D1
Longdon Green 56 D1
Longfield 54 B6
Longfield 55 H5
Longfield Hill 55 H5
Longford *Gt.Lon.* **54 B4**
Longford *Tel. & W.* **56 A1**
Longford *W.Mid.* **57 G4**
Longforgan 37 E3
Longhope *Glos.* 12 B4
Longhope *Ork.* 45 B4
Longhoughton 33 H5
Longlands 55 F4
Longniddry 32 D2
Longridge *Lancs.* 22 D3
Longridge *Staffs.* **56 C1**
Longshaw 58 D2
Longside 41 G3
Longstanton 14 C1
Longton 22 C3
Longtown 27 H2
Looe 4 B6
Loose 9 E3
Loscoe 19 E2
Lossiemouth 40 C2
Lostock Gralam 22 D6
Lostock Gralam 59 E5
Lostock Green 59 E5
Lostock Junction 59 E2
Lostwithiel 4 B6
Loth 45 D2
Loudwater 54 A2
Loughborough 19 F4
Loughor 11 E5
Loughton 14 C5
Loughton 55 F2
Louth 25 G5
Loves Green 55 H1
Low Habberley 56 B5
Lowdham 19 F2
Lower Ashtead 54 C6
Lower Beeding 8 B4
Lower Bentley 56 C6
Lower Bredbury 59 H3
Lower Cam 12 C4
Lower Clent 56 C4
Lower Edmonton 55 E2
Lower Green 56 C2
Lower Halstow 15 E6
Lower Heath 59 G6
Lower Kersal 59 F2
Lower Kingswood 54 D6
Lower Kinnerton 58 B6
Lower Nazeing 55 E1
Lower Penn 56 B3
Lower Peover 59 F5
Lower Shuckburgh 57 H6
Lower Stonnall 56 D2
Lower Stretton 59 E4
Lower Walton 59 E4
Lower Whitley 59 E5
Lower Withington 59 G6
Lowestoft 21 H4
Loweswater 27 G4
Lowsonford 57 E6
Lowton 59 E3
Lowton Common 59 E3
Loxwood 8 A4
Luddenden Foot 23 F3
Luddesdown 55 H5
Ludgershall 7 E2
Ludlow 12 B1
Ludstone 56 B3
Lullington 57 F1
Lumphanan 41 E5
Lumsden 40 D4
Lunan 37 F2
Lunanhead 37 E2
Luncarty 36 C3
Lundin Links 37 E4
Lunna 45 H3
Lunt 58 B2
Lusta 38 A3
Luthermuir 37 F1

Luthrie 37 E4
Luton 14 A3
Lutterworth 19 F5
Luxulyan 3 H4
Lybster 43 G4
Lydd 9 F4
Lydford 4 D4
Lydgate
   (Littleborough) 59 H1
Lydgate (Oldham) 59 H2
Lydiard Millicent 12 D5
Lydiate 22 C4
Lydiate 58 B2
Lydney 12 B4
Lye 56 C4
Lye Green *Bucks.* **54 A1**
Lye Green *Warks.* **57 E6**
Lyme Regis 6 A5
Lyminge 9 G3
Lymington 7 F5
Lymm 22 D5
Lymm 59 E4
Lympne 9 G4
Lympstone 5 F4
Lyndhurst 7 F4
Lyne 54 B5
Lyneham 12 D6
Lynemouth 28 D1
Lyness 45 C4
Lynmouth 5 E1
Lynn 56 A1
Lynton 5 E1
Lytchett Matravers 6 D5
Lytham St. Anne's 22 C3

M

Mablethorpe 25 H5
Macclesfield 23 F6
Macclesfield 59 H5
Macclesfield Forest 59 H5
Macduff 41 F2
Machrihanish 30 C5
Machynlleth 16 D5
Madeley *Staffs.* 18 B2
Madeley *Tel. & W.* **56 A2**
Madley 12 A3
Madron 3 E5
Maenclochog 10 B3
Maerdy *Denb.* 17 E3
Maerdy *R.C.T.* 11 G5
Maes-hafn 58 A6
Maesteg 11 F5
Magdalen Laver 55 G1
Maghull 22 C4
Maghull 58 B2
Magor 12 A5
Maidenhead 13 H5
Maidstone 9 E3
Major's Green 57 E5
Malden Rushett 54 C5
Maldon 15 E4
Mallaig (Malaig) 38 D2
Malmesbury 12 D5
Malpas 17 G3
Maltby 24 C5
Malton 24 D1
Manby 25 G5
Mancetter 19 E5
Mancetter 57 G3
Manchester 23 E5
Manchester 59 G3
Manchester Airport 59 G4
Mancot Royal 58 B6
Manea 20 B5
Manley 58 D5
Manningtree 15 F3
Manor Park 54 A3
Manorbier 10 B5
Mansfield 24 C6
Mansfield
   Woodhouse 24 C6
Manston *Dorset* 6 C4
Manston *Kent* 15 H6
Maple Cross 54 B2
Maplescombe 55 G5
Mappleborough
   Green 57 E6
Marazion 3 F5
March 20 B5

Marcham 13 F5
Marchington 18 D3
Marchwiel 17 G3
Marchwood 7 F4
Marden *Here.* 12 B2
Marden *Kent* 9 E3
Marden Ash 55 G1
Maresfield 8 C4
Margaretting 55 H1
Margaretting Tye 55 H1
Margate 15 H6
Marham 20 D4
Mark 6 A2
Market Bosworth 57 H2
Market Deeping 20 A4
Market Drayton 18 A3
Market Harborough 19 G5
Market Lavington 6 D2
Market Rasen 25 F5
Market Warsop 24 C6
Market Weighton 24 D2
Markfield 19 E4
Markfield 57 H1
Markinch 36 D4
Marks Gate 55 F2
Marks Tey 15 F3
Markyate 14 A4
Marland 59 G1
Marlborough 13 E6
Marlbrook 56 C5
Marldon 5 E5
Marlow 13 H5
Marnhull 6 C4
Marple 23 F5
Marple 59 H4
Marple Bridge 59 H4
Marsden 23 F4
Marsh Green 58 D2
Marshalswick 54 C1
Marshfield *Newport* 11 H5
Marshfield *S.Glos.* 12 C6
Marshside 58 B1
Marske-by-the-Sea 29 F4
Marsland Green 59 E3
Marston
   Ches.W. & C. **59 E5**
Marston *Staffs.* **56 B1**
Marston *Warks.* **57 F3**
Marston Green 57 E4
Marston Moretaine 14 A2
Marthall 59 F5
Martham 21 G4
Martin Hussingtree 56 B6
Martinscroft 59 E4
Martlesham 15 G2
Martlesham Heath 15 G2
Martley 12 C1
Martock 6 A4
Marton *Ches.E.* **59 G6**
Marton *Warks.* **57 H6**
Martyr's Green 54 B6
Maryburgh
   (Baile Màrtainn) 39 H3
Marykirk 37 F1
Marylebone
   Gt.Lon. **54 D3**
Marylebone
   Gt.Man. **58 D2**
Maryport 27 F4
Marywell 37 F2
Matchborough 56 D6
Matlock 24 B6
Matlock Bath 18 D1
Mattishall 21 E4
Mauchline 31 H5
Maud 41 G3
Maulden 14 A3
Mavesyn Ridware 56 D1
Mawdesley 58 C1
Maxstoke 57 F4
Maybole 31 G6
Maybury 54 B6
Mayfair 54 D3
Mayfield *E.Suss.* 8 D4
Mayfield *Midloth.* 32 D2
Mayfield *Staffs.* 18 D2
Mayford 54 A6
Maylandsea 15 F4
Meare 6 A2

Measham 19 E4
Measham 57 G1
Meden Vale 24 C6
Medstead 7 G3
Meer End 57 F5
Meerbrook 59 H6
Meigle 36 D2
Meikleour 36 D3
Melbost 44 E3
Melbourn 14 C2
Melbourne 19 E3
Meldreth 14 C2
Melksham 12 D6
Melling 22 C4
Melling 58 B2
Melling Mount 58 C2
Mellor 23 D3
Mellor 59 H4
Melrose 33 E4
Meltham 23 F4
Melton 15 G2
Melton Mowbray 19 G4
Melvaig 38 D1
Melvich 43 E2
Memsie 41 G2
Memus 37 E2
Menai Bridge
   (Porthaethwy) 16 C2
Mendlesham 15 G1
Menheniot 4 B5
Menithwood 56 A6
Menston 24 A2
Menstrie 32 A1
Meopham 14 D6
Meopham 55 H5
Meopham Green 55 H5
Meppershall 14 B3
Mere *Ches.E.* **59 F4**
Mere *Wilts.* 6 C3
Mere Brow 58 C1
Mere Green 57 E3
Mere Heath 59 E5
Mereworth 55 H6
Meriden 18 D5
Meriden 57 F4
Merley 6 D5
Merriott 6 A4
Merrow 54 B6
Merry Hill 54 C2
Merry Hill
   (Brierley Hill) 56 C4
Merry Hill
   (Wolverhampton)
   56 B3
Mersham 9 F4
Merstham 54 D6
Merthyr Tydfil 11 G4
Merthyr Vale 11 G5
Messingham 24 D4
Metheringham 25 E6
Methil 32 D1
Methlick 41 F4
Methven 36 C3
Methwold 20 D5
Mevagissey 3 H4
Mexborough 24 B5
Mey 43 G2
Miavaig (Miabhaig) 44 C3
Mickle Trafford 22 C6
Mickle Trafford 58 C6
Micklefield Green 54 B2
Mickleham 54 C6
Micklehurst 59 H2
Mickleton 13 E2
Mickletown 24 B3
Mid Calder 32 B2
Mid Yell 45 J2
Middle Barton 13 F3
Middle Bickenhill 57 F4
Middle Rasen 25 E5
Middlesbrough 29 E4
Middlestown 24 A4
Middleton *Gt.Man.* 23 E4
Middleton *Norf.* 20 C4
Middleton Cheney 13 F2
Middleton St. George 29 E5
Middleton-in-Teesdale
   28 C4

Middleton-on-Sea 8 A6
Middlewich 23 E6
Middlewich 59 F6
Middlewood 59 H4
Midhurst 7 H3
Midsomer Norton 6 B2
Midtown 38 D1
Milborne Port 6 B4
Mildenhall 15 E1
Milford 8 A3
Milford Haven
   (Aberdaugleddau) 10 B4
Milford on Sea 7 E5
Mill Brow 59 H4
Mill Green *Essex* **55 H1**
Mill Green *Herts.* **54 D1**
Mill Green *W.Mid.* **56 D2**
Mill Hill 54 D2
Mill Street 55 H6
Millbrook 4 D7
Miller's Green 55 G1
Millom 27 G6
Millport 31 F4
Milltimber 41 F5
Milltown of Edinvillie 40 C3
Milltown of
   Rothiemay 41 E3
Milnathort 36 D4
Milners Heath 58 C6
Milngavie 31 H3
Milnrow 23 F4
Milnrow 59 H1
Milnthorpe 27 H6
Milton *Cambs.* 14 C1
Milton *High.* 40 A2
Milton
   (Baile a' Mhuilinn) 39 G4
Milton Keynes 13 H3
Milton of Balgonie 37 E4
Milton of Campsie 31 H3
Milton-under-Wychwood
   13 F4
Milverton *Som.* 5 G2
Milverton *Warks.* **57 G6**
Mimbridge 54 A5
Minard 31 E2
Minchinhampton 12 C4
Minehead 5 F1
Minety 12 D5
Minster (Sheppey)
   Kent 15 F6
Minster (Thanet)
   Kent 15 H6
Minster Lovell 13 F4
Minsterley 17 G3
Mintlaw 41 G3
Minworth 57 E3
Mirfield 24 A3
Misterton 24 D5
Mistley 15 G3
Mitcham 54 D5
Mitcheldean 12 B4
Mitton 56 B1
Mobberley 23 E6
Mobberley 59 F5
Mochdre 16 D2
Modbury 4 D6
Moelfre 16 C1
Moffat 32 B5
Moira 57 G1
Mold (Yr Wyddgrug) 22 B6
Mollington 58 B5
Moniaive 27 E1
Monifieth 37 E3
Monken Hadley 54 D2
Monks Kirby 57 H4
Monks' Heath 59 G5
Monmouth
   (Trefynwy) 12 B4
Montgarrie 41 E5
Montgomery
   (Trefaldwyn) 17 F6
Montrose 37 G2
Monymusk 41 E5
Moodiesburn 31 H3
Moons Moat North 56 D6
Moor Green 56 D4
Moore 58 D4

Moorends 24 C4
Moorside 59 H2
Morar 38 C6
Morden 54 D5
Morden Park 54 D5
Morecambe 22 C1
Moresby Parks 27 F5
Moreton *Essex* 55 G1
Moreton *Mersey.* 58 A4
Moreton *Staffs.* 56 A1
Moreton-in-Marsh 13 E3
Moretonhampstead 5 E4
Morley 24 A3
Morley Green 59 G4
Morpeth 28 D1
Morrey 57 E1
Mortehoe 4 C1
Mortimer 13 G6
Mortlake 54 D4
Morton (Bourne)
 Lincs. 20 A3
Morton (Gainsborough)
 Lincs. 24 D5
Morton Bagot 57 E6
Morwenstow 4 B3
Moseley 56 C3
Moses Gate 57 F2
Moss Bank 58 D3
Moss Houses 59 G5
Moss Nook 59 G4
Moss Side *Gt.Man.* 59 G3
Moss Side *Mersey.* 58 B2
Mossbank 45 H3
Mossblown 31 G5
Mossley *Ches.E.* 59 G6
Mossley *Gt.Man.* 23 F4
Mossley *Gt.Man.* 59 H2
Mossley Hill 58 B4
Mosstodloch 40 D2
Mossy Lea 58 D1
Moston 59 G2
Moston Green 59 F6
Mostyn 22 B5
Motherwell 32 A3
Mottingham 55 F4
Mottram St. Andrew
 59 G5
Mottram in Longdendale
 59 H3
Mouldsworth 58 D5
Moulin 36 C2
Moulton
 Ches.W. & C. 22 D6
Moulton
 Ches.W. & C. 59 E6
Moulton *Lincs.* 20 B3
Moulton
 W.N'hants. 13 H1
Mount Hawke 3 G4
Mount Manisty 58 B5
Mount Pleasant
 Derbys. 57 F1
Mount Pleasant
 Flints. 58 A5
Mount Pleasant
 Gt.Lon. 54 B2
Mountain Ash
 (Aberpennar) 11 G5
Mountnessing 55 H2
Mountsorrel 19 F4
Moxley 56 C3
Much Hadham 14 C4
Much Hoole 22 C3
Much Wenlock 18 A5
Mucking 55 H3
Muckley Corner 56 D2
Mugswell 54 D6
Muir of Ord
 (Am Blàr Dubh) 39 H3
Muirhead 37 E3
Muirkirk 31 H5
Muirton 36 C4
Mulbarton 21 F4
Mullion 3 F6
Mundesley 21 G3
Mundford 20 D5
Munlochy 39 H3
Murthly 36 C3
Murton 29 E3

Musselburgh 32 D2
Mustow Green 56 B5
Muthill 36 B4
Muxton 56 A1
Mylor Bridge 3 G5
Mytholmroyd 23 F3

N

Nafferton 25 E2
Nailsea 12 A6
Nailstone 57 H2
Nailsworth 12 C5
Nairn 40 A3
Nanpean 3 H4
Nantwich 18 A2
Naphill 13 H5
Napton on the Hill 57 H6
Narberth (Arberth) 10 C4
Narborough *Leics.* 19 F5
Narborough *Norf.* 20 D4
Nash Street 55 H5
Navenby 19 H2
Navestock 55 G2
Navestock Side 55 G2
Nazeing 55 F1
Neal's Green 57 G4
Neasden 54 D3
Neath (Castell-nedd) 11 F5
Necton 20 D4
Nedd 42 B4
Needham Market 15 F2
Needingworth 14 C1
Nefyn 16 B3
Neilston 31 G4
Nelson *Caerp.* 11 H5
Nelson *Lancs.* 23 E3
Nercwys 58 A6
Ness 58 B5
Neston 22 B6
Neston 58 A5
Nether Alderley 59 G5
Nether Dallachy 40 D2
Nether Heyford 13 G2
Nether Langwith 24 C6
Nether Stowey 5 G2
Nether Whitacre 57 F3
Netherseal 57 F1
Netherton
 Ches.W. & C. 58 D5
Netherton *Mersey.*
 58 B2
Netherton *W.Mid.* 56 C4
Netherton *W.Yorks.* 24 A4
Nethertown 57 E1
Nethy Bridge 40 B4
Netley Abbey 7 F4
Netley Marsh 7 F4
Nettleham 25 E6
Nettlestead 15 H6
Nettlestead Green 55 H6
New Abbey 27 F2
New Aberdour 41 F2
New Addington 55 E5
New Addington 14 C6
New Addington 55 E5
New Alresford 7 G3
New Arley 57 F3
New Ash Green 14 D6
New Ash Green 55 H5
New Barn 55 H5
New Brighton
 Flints. 58 A6
New Brighton
 Mersey. 58 B3
New Byth 41 F3
New Cross 58 B4
New Cumnock 31 H6
New Deer 41 F3
New Eltham 55 F4
New End 56 D6
New Farnley 24 A3
New Ferry 58 B4
New Galloway 26 D2
New Greens 54 C1
New Haw 55 B5
New Invention 56 C2
New Lane 58 C1
New Lane End 59 E3
New Leeds 41 G3
New Luce 26 B2

New Malden 54 D5
New Marske 29 F4
New Mills 23 F5
New Milton 7 E5
New Mistley 15 G3
New Ollerton 24 C6
New Oscott 56 D3
New Pitsligo 41 F3
New Quay 10 D1
New Romney 9 F4
New Rossington 24 C5
New Stevenston 32 A3
New Swannington 57 H1
New Tredegar 11 H4
Newark-on-Trent 19 G2
Newarthill 32 A3
Newbiggin-by-the-Sea
 29 E1
Newbold 57 H1
Newbold Verdon 19 E4
Newbold Verdon 57 H2
Newbold on Avon 57 H5
Newborough 20 A4
Newbridge
 (Cefn Bychan) 11 H5
Newburgh *Aber.* 41 G4
Newburgh *Fife* 36 D4
Newburgh *Lancs.* 58 C1
Newbury 13 F6
Newbury Park 55 F3
Newby Bridge 27 H6
Newcastle Emlyn (Castell
 Newydd Emlyn) 10 D2
Newcastle upon
 Tyne 28 D2
Newcastle-under-Lyme
 18 B2
Newchurch 7 G5
Newent 12 C3
Newgate Street 55 E1
Newhaven 8 C5
Newhey 59 H1
Newick 8 C4
Newington 15 E6
Newmachar 41 F5
Newmains 32 A3
Newmarket 14 D1
Newmill 40 D3
Newmilns 31 H5
Newney Green 55 H1
Newnham 12 B4
Newnham Paddox 57 H4
Newport *E.Riding* 24 D3
Newport *Essex* 14 D3
Newport *High.* 43 G4
Newport *I.o.W.* 7 G5
Newport *Tel. & W.* 18 B4
Newport *Tel. & W.* 56 A1
Newport
 (Casnewydd) 12 A5
Newport
 (Trefdraeth) 10 B3
Newport Pagnell 13 H2
Newport-on-Tay 37 E3
Newquay 3 G3
Newsbank 59 G6
Newstead 19 F2
Newton
 Ches.W. & C. 58 D5
Newton *Gt.Man.* 59 H3
Newton Abbot 5 E4
Newton Aycliffe 28 D4
Newton Burgoland 57 G2
Newton Ferrers 4 D6
Newton Longville 13 H3
Newton Poppleford 5 F4
Newton Regis 57 F2
Newton Stewart 26 C2
Newton with Scales 22 C3
Newton-le-Willows 22 D5
Newton-le-Willows
 58 D3
Newtongrange 32 D2
Newtonhill 41 G6
Newtonmore (Baile Ùr an
 t-Slèibh) 40 A6
Newtown *Bucks.* 54 A1
Newtown *Derbys.* 59 H4
Newtown
 (Great Wyrley) 56 C2

Newtown (Rushton
 Spencer) 59 H6
Newtown (Swinton) 59 F2
Newtown (Wigan) 58 D2
Newtown
 (Y Drenewydd) 17 F6
Newtown
 St. Boswells 33 E4
Newtown Unthank 57 H2
Newtyle 36 D2
Newyears Green 54 B3
Neyland 10 B4
Nine Ashes 55 G1
Ninfield 9 E5
Nizels 55 G6
No Man's Heath 57 F2
Noah's Ark 55 G6
Noak Hill 55 G2
Norbury 55 E4
Norcott Brook 59 E4
Norden 59 G1
Norley 58 D5
Normandy 54 A6
Normanton 24 B3
Normanton le Heath
 57 G1
Norris Hill 57 G1
North Acton 54 D3
North Anston 24 C5
North Ascot 54 A5
North Baddesley 7 F3
North Ballachulish (Baile a'
 Chaolais a Tuath) 35 F1
North Benfleet 15 E5
North Berwick 33 E1
North Bradley 6 C2
North Cave 24 D3
North Cornelly 11 F5
North Cray 55 F4
North Curry 6 A3
North Elmham 21 E3
North Erradale 38 D1
North Ferriby 25 E3
North Hillington 54 B3
North Kessock 39 H3
North Leigh 13 F4
North Molton 5 E2
North Mundham 7 H4
North Ockendon 55 G3
North Petherton 5 G2
North Rode 59 G6
North Roe 45 H2
North Shields 29 E2
North Somercotes 25 G5
North Stifford 55 H3
North Sunderland 33 H4
North Tawton 4 D3
North Thoresby 25 F5
North Walsham 21 F3
North Weald Bassett 14 C4
North Weald Bassett
 55 F1
North Wembley 54 C3
North Wingfield 24 B6
North Wootton 20 C3
Northallerton 29 E6
Northam 4 C2
Northampton 13 H1
Northaw 54 D1
Northbay 44 B9
Northborough 20 A4
Northchurch 54 A1
Northfield 56 D5
Northfleet 14 D6
Northfleet 55 H4
Northiam 9 E4
Northleach 13 E4
Northmuir 37 E2
Northolt 54 C3
Northop
 (Llaneurgain) 22 B6
Northop
 (Llaneurgain) 58 A6
Northop Hall 58 A6
Northowram 23 H4
Northton
 (Taobh Tuath) 44 C5
Northwich 22 D6
Northwich 59 E5

Northwood
 Gt.Lon. 54 B2
Northwood *I.o.W.* 7 F5
Northwood
 Mersey. 58 C3
Northwood Hills 54 C2
Norton *Halton* 58 D4
Norton *N.Yorks.* 24 D1
Norton *S.Yorks.* 24 C4
Norton *Shrop.* 56 A2
Norton *W.Mid.* 56 B4
Norton Canes 18 C4
Norton Canes 56 D2
Norton Fitzwarren 5 G2
Norton Heath 55 H1
Norton Lindsey 57 F6
Norton Mandeville 55 G1
Norton-Juxta-Twycross
 57 G2
Norwich 21 F4
Norwood End 55 G1
Norwood Green 54 C4
Notting Hill 54 D3
Nottingham 19 F2
Noutard's Green 56 A6
Nuneaton 19 E5
Nuneaton 57 G3
Nursling 7 F4
Nurton 56 B3
Nutfield 55 E6
Nuthall 19 F2
Nuthurst 57 E5

O

Oadby 19 F4
Oakdale 11 H5
Oaken 56 B2
Oakengates 56 A1
Oakenholt 58 A5
Oakgrove 59 H6
Oakham 19 G4
Oakington 14 C1
Oaklands 14 B4
Oakley *Bed.* 14 A2
Oakley *Fife* 32 B1
Oakley *Hants.* 7 G2
Oakley Green 54 A4
Oakthorpe 57 G1
Oathlaw 37 E2
Oban (An t-Òban) 35 E3
Occlestone Green 59 E6
Ockeridge 56 A6
Ockham 54 B6
Odiham 7 H2
Odstone 57 G2
Offchurch 57 G6
Offenham 12 D2
Offerton 59 H4
Offham 55 H6
Oglet 58 C4
Ogmore Vale 11 G5
Ogmore-by-Sea 11 F6
Okehampton 4 D4
Old Arley 18 D5
Old Arley 57 F3
Old Basing 7 G2
Old Buckenham 21 E5
Old Cleeve 5 F1
Old Deer 41 G3
Old Ford 55 E3
Old Hill 56 C4
Old Kilpatrick 31 G3
Old Leake 20 B2
Old Milverton 57 F6
Old Rayne 41 E4
Old Stratford 13 H2
Old Swinford 56 C4
Old Windsor 14 A6
Old Windsor 54 A4
Old Woking 54 B6
Olderberrow 57 E6
Oldbury *Kent* 55 G6
Oldbury *Shrop.* 56 A3
Oldbury *W.Mid.* 18 C5
Oldbury *W.Mid.* 56 C4
Oldbury *Warks.* 57 G3
Oldfield 56 B6
Oldham 23 F4
Oldham 59 H2

Oldham Edge 59 H2
Oldmeldrum 41 F4
Oldwich Lane 57 F5
Ollaberry 45 H2
Ollerton Ches.E. 59 F5
Ollerton Notts. 24 C6
Olney 13 H2
Olton 57 E4
Olveston 12 B5
Ombersley 12 C1
Ombersley 56 B6
Onchan 26 C6
Onich (Omhanaich) 35 F1
Onllwyn 11 F4
Ordie 40 D5
Orford Suff. 15 H2
Orford Warr. 59 E3
Orgreave 57 E1
Ormesby
   St. Margaret 21 G4
Ormiston 32 D2
Ormskirk 22 C4
Ormskirk 58 C2
Orpington 14 C6
Orpington 59 F5
Orrell Gt.Man. 22 D4
Orrell Gt.Man. 58 D2
Orrell Mersey. 58 B3
Orsett 14 D5
Orsett 55 H3
Orsett Heath 55 H3
Orslow 58 B1
Orton-on-the-Hill 57 G2
Osbaston 57 H2
Osbaston Hollow 57 H2
Oscroft 58 D6
Osgathorpe 57 H1
Ossett 24 A3
Osterley 54 C4
Oswaldtwistle 23 E3
Oswestry 17 F4
Otford 8 D3
Otford 55 G6
Otherton 56 C1
Otley 24 A2
Otterbourne 7 F3
Otterburn 28 B1
Ottershaw 54 A5
Ottery St. Mary 5 F4
Oughtibridge 24 B5
Oundle 19 H5
Ouston 28 D3
Outwell 20 C4
Outwoods 56 A1
Over 14 C1
Over 59 E6
Over Green 57 E3
Over Hulton 59 E2
Over Peover 59 F5
Over Tabley 59 F4
Over Wallop 7 E3
Over Whitacre 57 F3
Overbister 45 D1
Overcombe 6 B5
Overpool 58 B5
Overseal 57 F1
Overslade 57 H5
Overton
   Ches.W. & C. 58 D5
Overton Hants. 7 G2
Overton (Owrtyn) 17 G3
Overtown 32 A3
Oxford 13 G4
Oxhey 54 C2
Oxley 56 C2
Oxshott 14 B6
Oxshott 54 C5
Oxted 8 C3
Oxted 55 E6
Oxton 58 B4
Oyne 41 E4

P

Packington 57 G1
Packwood 57 E5
Paddington 58 D3
Paddock Wood 8 D3
Padeswood 58 A6

Padiham 23 E3
Padstow 3 H3
Pagham 7 H5
Paignton 5 E5
Pailton 57 H4
Painshawfield 28 C2
Painswick 12 C4
Paisley 31 G3
Pakenham 15 F1
Palmers Green 55 E2
Panbride 37 F3
Pangbourne 13 G6
Pannal 24 B2
Pant 17 F4
Papworth Everard 14 B1
Par 3 H4
Parbold 22 C4
Parbold 58 C1
Park End 56 A5
Park Gate 56 C5
Park Langley 55 E5
Park Street 54 C1
Parkeston 15 G3
Parkfield 56 C3
Parkgate 58 A5
Partington 23 E5
Partington 59 F3
Parton 27 F4
Partridge Green 8 B5
Paslow Wood
   Common 55 G1
Passingford Bridge 55 G2
Patchetts Green 54 C2
Patchway 12 B5
Pateley Bridge 24 A1
Patna 31 G6
Patrington 25 G3
Pattingham 18 B5
Pattingham 56 B3
Pattishall 13 G2
Paulton 6 B2
Pave Lane 56 A1
Paxton 33 G3
Peacehaven 8 C5
Peartree Green 55 G2
Peasedown St. John 6 C2
Peasley Cross 58 D3
Peat Inn 37 E4
Peathill 41 G2
Pebble Coombe 54 D6
Peckham 55 E4
Peckleton 57 H2
Pedmore 56 C4
Peebles 32 C3
Peel 26 B5
Peggs Green 57 H1
Pegswood 28 D1
Pelsall 56 D2
Pelton 28 D3
Pelynt 4 B6
Pemberton 58 D2
Pembrey (Pen-bre) 10 D4
Pembroke (Penfro) 10 B4
Pembroke Dock
   (Doc Penfro) 10 B4
Pembury 8 D3
Pen-clawdd 11 E5
Pen-y-fai 11 F5
Pen-y-parc 58 A6
Penarth 11 H6
Pencaitland 32 D2
Pencoed 11 G5
Pendine Pentywyn 10 C4
Pendlebury 23 E4
Pendlebury 59 F2
Penge 55 E4
Penicuik 32 C2
Penistone 24 A4
Penketh 58 D4
Penkridge 18 C4
Penkridge 56 C1
Penmaenmawr 16 D2
Penn Bucks. 14 A2
Penn W.Mid. 56 B3
Penn Street 54 A2
Pennan 41 F2
Pennington Green 59 E2
Penrhiwceiber 11 G5
Penrhyn Bay
   (Bae Penrhyn) 16 D1

Penrhyndeudraeth 16 C4
Penrith 28 A4
Penryn 3 G5
Pensax 56 A6
Pensby 58 A4
Penshaw 29 E3
Pensilva 4 B5
Pensnett 56 C4
Pentonville 55 E3
Pentre 11 G5
Pentre Ffwrndan 58 A5
Pentre Halkyn 58 A5
Pen-y-bont 11 H1
Penybontfawr 17 F3
Penycae 17 F3
Pen-y-ffordd 22 C6
Pen-y-ffordd 58 B6
Penygraig 11 G5
Pen-y-groes 16 B3
Penymynydd 58 B6
Penywaun 11 G4
Penzance 3 E5
Peover Heath 59 F5
Perivale 54 C3
Perranarworthal 3 G5
Perranporth 3 G4
Perry Barr 56 D3
Perry Crofts 57 F2
Perry Street 55 H4
Pershore 12 D2
Perth (Peairt) 36 D3
Perton 56 B3
Peterborough 20 A5
Peterculter 41 F5
Peterhead 41 H3
Peterlee 29 E3
Petersfield 7 H3
Peterston-super-Ely 11 G6
Petts Wood 55 F4
Petworth 8 A4
Pevensey Bay 8 D5
Pewsey 13 E6
Pickerells 55 G1
Pickering 29 G6
Pickford Green 57 F4
Pickmere 59 E5
Picton 58 C5
Pierowall 45 D1
Pilgrims Hatch 55 G2
Pillaton 58 C1
Pilling 22 C2
Pillowell 12 B4
Pilning 12 B5
Pilsley 24 B6
Pimhole 59 G1
Pimlico 54 B1
Pimperne 6 D4
Pinchbeck 20 A3
Pinfold 58 B1
Pinley Green 57 F6
Pinner 54 C3
Pinner Green 54 C2
Pinwherry 26 B1
Pinxton 19 E2
Pipe Ridware 56 D1
Pipehill 56 D2
Pirbright 54 A6
Pirton 43 E5
Pitcairngreen 36 C3
Pitcaple 41 F4
Pitch Place 54 A6
Pitlessie 37 E4
Pitlochry 36 C2
Pitmedden 41 F4
Pitscottie 37 E4
Pitsea 14 D4
Pitsford 19 E4
Pitstone 14 A4
Pittentrail 43 E5
Pittenweem 37 F4
Plains 32 A2
Plaistow 55 E3
Platt 55 H6
Platt Bridge 59 E2
Plaxtol 55 H6
Pleasley 24 C6
Pleck 56 C3
Plemstall 58 C5
Plockton (Am Ploc) 38 D4
Plough Hill 57 G3
Plumley 59 F5

Plumstead 55 F4
Plymouth 4 C6
Pocklington 24 D2
Polbain 42 A5
Polbeth 32 B2
Polegate 8 D5
Polesworth 18 D4
Polesworth 57 F2
Polglass 42 A5
Polgooth 3 H4
Polmont 32 B2
Polperro 4 B6
Ponders End 55 E2
Pontardawe 11 F4
Pontarddulais 11 E4
Pontblyddyn 58 A6
Pontefract 24 B3
Ponteland 28 D2
Pontesbury 17 G5
Pontllan-fraith 11 H5
Pontlliw 11 E4
Pontrhydfendigaid 11 F1
Pontyates (Pont-iets) 10 D4
Pontyberem 11 E4
Pontyclun 11 G5
Pontycymer 11 G5
Pontypool 11 H4
Pontypridd 11 G5
Pool 24 A2
Pool Green 56 D2
Pool of Muckhart 36 C4
Poole 6 D5
Poolewe 38 D1
Pooley Bridge 27 H4
Poplar 55 E3
Poringland 21 F4
Porlock 5 E1
Port Appin (Port na
   h-Apainn) 35 F2
Port Askaig 30 B3
Port Bannatyne 31 E3
Port Ellen 30 B4
Port Erin 26 B6
Port Erroll 41 G4
Port Eynon 10 D5
Port Glasgow 31 G3
Port St. Mary 26 B6
Port Sunlight 58 B4
Port Talbot 11 F5
Port William 26 C3
Port of Menteith 31 H1
Port of Ness
   (Port Nis) 44 F1
Portchester 7 G4
Portgordon 40 D2
Porth 11 G5
Porthcawl 11 F6
Porthleven 3 F5
Porthmadog 16 C4
Portishead 12 A6
Portknockie 40 D2
Portlethen 41 G6
Portlethen Village 41 G6
Portmahomack 40 B1
Portnacroish
   (Port na Croise) 35 F2
Portnaguran
   (Port nan Giúran) 44 F3
Portnahaven 30 A4
Portpatrick 26 A3
Portree (Port Righ) 38 B3
Portskerra 43 G2
Portskewett 12 B5
Portslade-by-Sea 8 B5
Portsmouth 7 G4
Portsonachan 35 F3
Portsoy 41 E2
Portway 56 D5
Pott Shrigley 59 H5
Potten End 54 B1
Potter Street 55 F1
Potter's Green 57 G4
Potterne 6 D2
Potters Bar 14 B4
Potters Bar 54 D1
Potters Crouch 54 C1
Potters Marston 57 H3
Potterspury 13 H2
Potterton 41 G4
Potton 14 B2

Poulton-le-Fylde 22 C3
Pound Green 56 A5
Powburn 33 G5
Powick 12 C2
Poyle 54 B4
Poynton 23 F5
Poynton 59 H4
Pratt's Bottom 55 F5
Prees 18 A3
Preesall 22 C2
Prenbrigog 58 A6
Prenton 58 B4
Prescot 22 C5
Prescot 58 C3
Prestatyn 22 A5
Prestbury Ches.E. 23 F6
Prestbury Ches.E. 59 H5
Prestbury Glos. 12 D3
Presteigne
   (Llanandras) 12 A1
Prestolee 59 F2
Preston Dorset 6 C5
Preston E.Riding 25 F3
Preston Lancs. 22 C5
Preston Bagot 57 E6
Preston Brook 58 D4
Preston on the Hill 58 D4
Prestonpans 32 D2
Prestwich 23 E4
Prestwich 59 G2
Prestwick 31 G5
Prestwood 13 H4
Priestwood 55 H5
Primrose Hill 54 D3
Princes End 56 C3
Princes Risborough 13 H4
Princethorpe 57 H5
Princetown 4 D5
Priorslee 56 A1
Probus 3 H4
Prudhoe 28 D2
Pucklechurch 12 B6
Puddinglake 59 F6
Puddington 58 B5
Pudsey 24 A3
Pulborough 8 A5
Purbrook 7 G4
Purfleet-on-Thames
   55 G4
Puriton 6 A2
Purleigh 15 E2
Purley 55 E5
Purton 12 D5
Putney 54 D4
Pwllheli 16 B4
Pye Green 56 C1
Pyle 11 F5
Pyrton 54 B6
Pyrford Green 54 B6

Q

Quainton 13 H4
Quarff 45 H5
Quarry Bank 56 C4
Quarrybank 58 D6
Quatford 56 A3
Quatt 56 A4
Quedgeley 12 C4
Queenborough 15 F6
Queensbury
   Gt.Lon. 54 C3
Queensbury W.Yorks. 24 A3
Queensferry 22 C6
Queensferry 58 B6
Queniborough 19 F4
Queslett 56 D3
Quinton 56 C4
Quorn 19 F4

R

Raby 58 B5
Radcliffe 23 E4
Radcliffe 59 F2
Radcliffe on Trent 19 F3
Radford 57 G4
Radford Semele 13 F1
Radford Semele 57 G6
Radlett 14 B4

Radlett 54 C1
Radley 13 G5
Radley Green 55 H1
Radstock 6 B2
Radyr 11 H5
Rafford 40 B3
Raglan 12 A4
Rain Shore 59 G1
Rainford 22 C4
Rainford 58 C2
Rainham 55 G3
Rainhill 58 C3
Rainhill Stoops 58 D3
Rainow 59 H5
Rainsough 59 F2
Rainworth 19 F2
Rait 36 D3
Rampton 24 D6
Ramsbottom 23 E4
Ramsbottom 59 F1
Ramsbury 13 E6
Ramsden Heath 15 E5
Ramsey *Cambs.* 20 A5
Ramsey *Essex* 15 G3
Ramsey *I.o.M.* 26 C5
Ramsgate 15 H6
Randwick 12 C4
Ranskill 24 C5
Rapness 45 D1
Rashwood 56 C6
Ratby 19 F4
Ratcliffe Culey 57 G3
Rathen 41 G2
Ratho 32 C2
Rathven 40 D2
Raunds 14 A1
Ravenshead 19 F2
Ravenstone 57 H1
Rawmarsh 24 B5
Rawnsley 56 D1
Rawtenstall 23 E3
Rayleigh 15 E5
Rayne 15 E3
Rayners Lane 54 C3
Raynes Park 54 D5
Read 23 E3
Reading 13 H6
Reawick 45 H4
Reay 43 F2
Red Lodge 14 D1
Red Lumb 59 G1
Red Rock 58 D2
Redbourn 14 B4
Redcar 29 F4
Reddish 59 G3
Redditch 12 D1
Redditch 56 D6
Redford 37 F2
Redhill 8 B3
Redhill 54 D6
Redlynch 7 E3
Redruth 3 G4
Reepham *Lincs.* 25 E6
Reepham *Norf.* 21 E3
Reigate 8 B3
Reigate 54 D6
Reiss 43 H3
Renfrew 31 H3
Renhold 14 A2
Renton 31 G3
Repton 19 E3
Resolven 11 F4
Retford 24 D5
Rettendon 15 E5
Reydon 15 H1
Rhayader
  (Rhaeadr Gwy) 11 G1
Rhoose 11 G6
Rhosesmor 58 A6
Rhosllanerchrugog 17 F3
Rhosneigr 16 B2
Rhostyllen 17 G3
Rhubodach 31 E3
Rhuddall Heath 58 D6
Rhuddlan 22 A6
Rhydymwyn 58 A6
Rhyl 22 A5
Rhymney 11 H4
Rhynd 36 D3

Rhynie 40 D4
Ribbesford 56 A5
Ribchester 22 D3
Riccall 24 C3
Richings Park 54 B4
Richmond *Gt.Lon.* 14 B6
Richmond Gt.Lon. 54 C4
Richmond *N.Yorks.* 28 D5
Rickmansworth 14 A5
Rickmansworth 54 B2
Riddlesden 23 F2
Ridge 54 D1
Ridge Lane 57 F3
Ridley 55 H5
Rileyhill 57 E1
Ring o' Bells 58 C1
Ringmer 8 C5
Ringstead 14 A1
Ringwood 7 E4
Ripley *Derbys.* 19 E2
Ripley Surr. 54 B6
Ripon 24 B1
Ripple 12 C3
Ripponden 23 F4
Risca 11 H5
Riseley 14 A1
Rishton 23 E3
Risley *Derbys.* 19 E3
Risley Warr. 59 E3
Riverhead 55 G6
Riverview Park 55 H4
Rivington 59 E1
Roade 13 H2
Roadside of Kinneff 37 G1
Robertsbridge 9 E4
Robin Hood 58 D1
Roby 58 C3
Roby Mill 58 D2
Rocester 18 D3
Rochdale 23 E4
Rochdale 59 G1
Roche 3 H3
Rochester 15 E6
Rochford 15 E5
Rock 56 A5
Rock Ferry 58 B4
Rockwell Green 5 G3
Rode Heath 18 B2
Rodeheath 59 G6
Rodney Stoke 6 A2
Roe Cross 59 H3
Roehampton 54 D4
Rogerstone 11 H5
Rogiet 12 A5
Rollesby 21 G4
Rolleston-on-Dove 18 D3
Rolvenden 9 E4
Romford 14 D5
Romford 55 G3
Romiley 23 F5
Romiley 59 H3
Romney Street 55 G5
Romsey 7 F3
Romsley Shrop. 56 A4
Romsley *Worcs.* 18 C5
Romsley Worcs. 56 C5
Rood End 56 D4
Ropley 7 G3
Rora 41 G3
Rosehearty 41 G2
Rosemarkie 40 A3
Rosemount 36 D2
Roseville 56 C3
Rosliston 57 F1
Ross-on-Wye 12 B3
Rossett 17 G3
Rossington 24 C5
Rostherne 59 F4
Rosyth 32 C1
Rothbury 33 G5
Rotherfield 9 E4
Rotherfield Peppard 13 H5
Rotherham 24 B5
Rothes 40 C3
Rothesay 31 E3
Rothienorman 41 F4
Rothley 19 F4
Rothwell
  N.N'hants. 19 G5
Rothwell *W.Yorks.* 24 B3

Rotten Row 57 E5
Rottingdean 8 C5
Roughley 57 E3
Roughton 56 A3
Round Bush 54 C2
Row Town 54 B5
Rowde 12 D6
Rowhedge 15 F3
Rowington 57 F6
Rowlands Gill 28 D3
Rowley Regis 56 C4
Rowney Green 56 D5
Rownhams 7 F4
Rowton 58 C6
Roxton 14 B2
Roxwell 14 D4
Roxwell 55 H1
Royal Leamington
  Spa 13 F1
Royal Leamington
  Spa 57 G6
Royal Oak 58 C2
Royal Tunbridge Wells 8 D4
Royal Wootton Bassett
  12 D5
Roybridge
  (Drochaid Ruaidh) 39 F6
Roydon (by Diss)
  Norf. 21 E5
Roydon (by King's Lynn)
  Norf. 20 D3
Roydon Hamlet 55 F1
Royston *Herts.* 14 C2
Royston *S.Yorks.* 24 B4
Royton 23 F4
Royton 59 H2
Ruabon (Rhiwabon) 17 G3
Ruardean 12 B4
Rubery 56 B5
Rucklers Lane 54 B1
Ruddington 19 F3
Rudgwick 8 A4
Rudheath 22 D6
Rudheath 59 E5
Rufford 22 C4
Rufford 58 C1
Rugby 13 G1
Rugeley 18 C4
Rugeley 56 D1
Ruishton 5 G2
Ruislip 55 B3
Ruislip Gardens 54 B3
Ruislip Manor 54 C3
Runcorn 22 D5
Runcorn 58 D4
Runshaw Moor 58 D1
Runwell 15 E5
Rush Green 55 G3
Rushall 56 D2
Rushden 14 A1
Rushgreen 59 E4
Rushmere
  St. Andrew 15 G2
Rushock 56 B5
Rusholme 59 G3
Rushton 58 D6
Rushton Spencer 59 H6
Rushwick 12 C2
Ruskington 19 H2
Rusper 8 B4
Ruspidge 12 B4
Rustington 8 A5
Rutherglen 31 H3
Ruthin (Rhuthun) 17 F3
Ruthven 41 E3
Ryarsh 55 H6
Ryde 7 G5
Rye 9 F4
Rye Park 55 E1
Ryhall 19 H4
Ryhill 24 B4
Ryton 28 D2
Ryton 56 A2
Ryton-on-Dunsmore
  57 G5

S

Sabden 23 E3
Sacriston 28 D3

Saffron Walden 14 D3
Saham Toney 20 D4
Saighton 58 C6
St. Agnes 3 G4
St. Albans 14 B4
St. Albans 54 C1
St. Andrews 37 F4
St. Anne 5 H5
St. Asaph (Llanelwy) 22 A6
St. Athan 11 G6
St. Austell 3 H4
St. Bees 27 F5
St. Blazey 3 H4
St. Boswells 33 E4
St. Brelade 5 G6
St. Briavels 12 B4
St. Brides Major 11 F6
St. Clears (Sanclêr) 10 C4
St. Cleer 4 B5
St. Columb Major 3 H3
St. Columb Road 3 H4
St. Combs 41 G2
St. Cyrus 37 G1
St. David's (Tyddewi) 10 A3
St. Day 3 G4
St. Dennis 3 H4
St. Dogmaels
  Llandudoch 10 C2
St. Erth 3 F5
St. Eval 3 G3
St. Fergus 41 H3
St. Fillans 36 A3
St. George's 56 A1
St. Germans 4 C6
St. Helens 22 D5
St. Helens 58 D3
St. Helier 5 H6
St. Helier 54 D5
St. Ives *Cambs.* 14 C1
St. Ives *Cornw.* 3 F4
St. Ives *Dorset* 7 E4
St. John 5 H6
St. John's Gt.Lon. 55 E4
St. John's Surr. 54 A6
St. John's Town of
  Dalry 26 D1
St. Just 3 E5
St. Just in Roseland 3 G5
St. Keverne 3 G5
St. Leonard's
  Street 55 H6
St. Leonards *Dorset* 7 E4
St. Leonards *E.Suss.* 9 E5
St. Leonards 54 A1
St. Margaret's Hope 45 D3
St. Margaret's at Cliffe 9 H3
St. Martin 5 H5
St. Martin's 17 G4
St. Mary Bourne 7 F2
St. Mary Cray 55 F5
St. Mary in the Marsh 9 F4
St. Mary's 45 C3
St. Mary's Bay 9 F4
St. Mawes 3 G5
St. Merryn 3 G3
St. Monans 37 F4
St. Neots 14 B2
St. Osyth 15 G4
St. Paul's Cray 55 F5
St. Peter Port 5 H5
St. Sampson 5 H5
St. Stephen 3 H4
St. Stephens 54 C1
St. Teath 3 H2
St. Vigeans 37 F2
Salcombe 5 E7
Sale 23 E5
Sale 59 F3
Salen *Arg. & B.* 34 D2
Salen *High.* 34 D1
Salford 23 E5
Salford 59 G3
Salford Priors 12 D2
Salfords 8 B3
Salhouse 21 G4
Saline 32 B1
Salisbury 7 E3
Salt Hill 54 A3
Saltash 4 C6
Saltburn 40 A2

Saltburn-by-the-Sea 29 F4
Saltcoats 31 F4
Saltdean 8 C5
Salterswall 59 E6
Saltford 12 B6
Saltley 56 D4
Saltney 58 B6
Salwarpe 56 B6
Sambourne 56 D6
Sanaigmore 30 A3
Sandbach 23 E6
Sandbach 59 F6
Sandend 41 E2
Sanderstead 55 E5
Sandford *Devon* 5 E3
Sandford *Dorset* 6 D5
Sandhaven 41 G2
Sandhurst *Brack.F.* 13 H6
Sandhurst *Kent* 9 E4
Sandiacre 19 E3
Sandiway 22 D6
Sandiway 59 E5
Sandlow Green 59 F6
Sandness 45 G4
Sandon 15 E4
Sandown 7 G5
Sandridge 14 B4
Sandwell 56 D4
Sandwich 9 H3
Sandwick 45 H5
Sandwick (Sanndabhaig)
  Na H-E.Siar 44 E3
Sandy 14 B2
Sandycroft 58 B6
Sankyn's Green 56 A6
Sanquhar 32 A5
Sapcote 19 E5
Sapcote 57 H3
Sapey Common 56 A6
Sarratt 14 A5
Sarratt 54 B2
Sauchen 41 E5
Saughall 22 C6
Saughall 58 B5
Saughall Massie 58 A4
Saundersfoot 10 C4
Sawbridgeworth 14 C4
Sawston 14 C2
Sawtry 20 A5
Saxilby 24 D6
Saxmundham 15 H1
Scalby 29 H6
Scalloway 45 H5
Scalpay 44 D5
Scarborough 29 H6
Scarcliffe 24 B6
Scarinish 34 A2
Scarisbrick 58 B1
Scarth Hill 58 C2
Scawby 25 E4
Scholes 24 B3
School Green 59 E6
Scole 15 G1
Scone 36 D3
Sconser 38 C4
Scotby 27 H3
Scotch Corner 28 D5
Scotlandwell 36 D4
Scotter 24 D4
Scotton 28 D6
Scourie 42 B3
Scousburgh 45 H6
Scouthead 59 H2
Scrabster 43 F2
Scremerston 33 G3
Scunthorpe 24 D4
Seacombe 58 A3
Seaford 8 C6
Seaforth 58 B3
Seaham 29 E3
Seahouses 33 H4
Seal 8 D3
Seal 55 G6
Sealand 58 B6
Seamer 29 H6
Seascale 27 F5
Seaton *Cumb.* 27 F4
Seaton *Devon* 5 G4
Seaton Delaval 29 E2
Seaton Sluice 29 E2

Seaview 7 G5
Seckington 57 F2
Sedbergh 28 A6
Sedbury 12 B5
Sedgefield 29 E4
Sedgemere 57 F5
Sedgley 56 C3
Sedlescombe 9 E5
Seend 12 D6
Seer Green 54 A2
Sefton 58 B2
Seghill 28 D2
Seisdon 56 B3
Selborne 7 H3
Selby 24 C3
Selhurst 55 E5
Selkirk 32 D4
Sellindge 9 F4
Selly Oak 56 D4
Selsdon 55 E5
Selsey 7 H5
Selston 19 E2
Send 8 A3
Send 54 B6
Send Marsh 54 B6
Sennybridge 11 G3
Settle 23 E1
Seven Kings 55 F3
Seven Sisters 11 F4
Sevenoaks 8 D3
Sevenoaks 55 G6
Sevenoaks Weald 55 G6
Severn Beach 12 B5
Sewardstone 55 E2
Sgiogarstaigh 44 F1
Shackerley 56 B2
Shackerstone 57 G2
Shadoxhurst 9 F4
Shaftesbury 6 C3
Shafton 24 B4
Shaldon 5 F5
Shalford 8 A3
Shanklin 7 G5
Shap 28 A5
Shard End 57 E4
Shareshill 56 C2
Sharlston 24 B4
Sharnbrook 14 A2
Sharnford 57 H3
Shatterford 56 A4
Shavington 18 A2
Shaw 23 F4
Shaw 59 H2
Shaw Side 59 H2
Shawbost (Siabost) 44 D2
Shawbury 18 A3
Shawfield 59 G1
Sheepy Magna 57 G2
Sheepy Parva 57 G2
Sheering 14 D4
Sheerness 15 F6
Sheffield 24 B5
Shefford 14 B3
Sheldon 57 E4
Shelf 24 A3
Shelfield W.Mid. 56 D2
Shelfield Warks. 57 E6
Shelfield Green 57 E6
Shellbrook 57 G1
Shelley 24 A4
Shelley 55 G1
Shellow Bowells 55 H1
**Shelsley
  Beauchamp 56 A6**
Shelsley Walsh 56 A6
Shenfield 55 H2
Shenley 14 B5
Shenley 54 C1
Shenleybury 54 C1
Shenstone Staffs. 18 D4
Shenstone Staffs. 57 E2
**Shenstone
  Worcs. 56 B5**
**Shenstone
  Woodend 57 E2**
Shenton 57 G2
Shepherd's Bush 54 D4
Shepherdswell 9 G3
Shepley 24 A4
Shepperton 14 A6

Shepperton 54 B5
Shepshed 19 E4
Shepshed 57 H1
Shepton Mallet 6 B2
Sherborne 6 B4
Sherborne St. John 7 G2
Sherbourne 57 F6
Sherburn 29 E3
Sherburn in Elmet 24 B3
Shere 8 A3
Sherfield on Loddon 7 G2
Sheriffhales 56 A1
Sheringham 21 F2
Shernal Green 56 C6
Sherston 12 C5
Shevington 22 D4
Shevington 58 D2
Shevington Moor 58 D1
Shieldaig 38 D3
Shieldhill 32 A2
Shifnal 18 B4
Shifnal 56 A2
Shilbottle 33 H5
Shildon 28 D4
Shillington 14 B3
Shilton 57 H4
Shiney Row 29 E3
Shinfield 13 H6
Shipbourne 55 G6
Shipbrookhill 59 E5
Shipdham 21 E4
Shipham 6 A2
Shiplake 13 H6
Shipley Shrop. 56 B3
Shipley W.Yorks. 24 A3
Shipston on Stour 13 E2
Shipton Bellinger 7 E2
Shipton-under-Wychwood
  13 E4
Shirdley Hill 58 B1
Shire Oak 56 D2
Shirebrook 24 C6
Shiremoor 29 E2
Shirenewton 12 A5
Shirland 19 E2
Shirley Gt.Lon. 55 E5
Shirley W.Mid. 57 E5
Shirley Heath 57 E5
Shooter's Hill 55 F4
Shore 59 H1
Shoreditch 55 E3
Shoreham 14 D6
Shoreham 55 G5
Shoreham-by-Sea 8 B5
Shorne 14 D6
Shorne 55 H4
Shorne Ridgeway 55 H4
**Short Heath
  Derbys. 57 G1**
**Short Heath
  W.Mid. 56 D3**
Shortlands 55 E5
Shotley 15 G3
Shotley Gate 15 G3
Shotton 22 C6
Shotton 58 B6
Shotton Colliery 29 E3
Shotts 32 A2
Shotwick 58 B5
Shrawley 56 B6
Shreding Green 54 B3
Shrewley 57 F6
Shrewsbury 17 G5
Shrewton 6 D2
Shrivenham 13 E5
Shurdington 12 D4
Shurnock 56 D6
Shustoke 57 F3
Shutt Green 56 B2
Shuttington 57 F2
Shuttleworth 59 F1
Sible Hedingham 15 E3
Sibsey 20 B2
Sibson 57 G2
Sidcup 55 F4
Siddington 12 D5
Siddington 59 G5
Sidemoor 56 C5
Sidlesham 7 H5
Sidmouth 5 G4

Silchester 13 G6
Sileby 19 F4
Silloth 27 G3
Silsden 23 F2
Silsoe 14 A3
Silver End 15 E4
Silverdale 22 C1
Silverstone 13 G2
Silverton 5 F3
Simister 59 G2
Simonsbath 5 E2
Singlewell 55 H4
Sinton Green 56 B6
Sipson 54 B4
Sittingbourne 15 F6
Six Ashes 56 A4
Skegness 25 H6
Skellingthorpe 25 E6
Skelmanthorpe 24 A4
Skelmersdale 22 C4
Skelmersdale 58 C2
Skelmorlie 31 F3
Skelton Cumb. 27 H4
Skelton R. & C. 29 F5
Skelton York 24 C2
Sketchley 57 H3
Skidby 25 E3
Skipton 23 F2
Skirlaugh 25 F3
Slade Green 55 G4
Slaithwaite 23 F4
Slamannan 32 A2
Sleaford 19 H2
Sleights 29 G5
Slinfold 8 B4
Slip End 14 A4
Slitting Mill 56 D1
Slough 14 A6
Slough 54 A3
Slyne 22 C1
Smailholm 33 E4
Smallbridge 59 H1
Smalley 19 E2
Smallfield 8 C3
Smallford 54 C1
Smarden 9 E3
Smestow 56 B3
Smethwick 18 C5
Smethwick 56 D4
Smethwick Green 59 G6
Smisby 57 G1
Smithton 40 A3
Smithy Green 59 F5
Smockington 57 H4
Snaith 24 C3
Snape Green 58 B1
Snarestone 57 G2
Snead's Green 56 B6
Snettisham 20 C3
Snitterfield 13 E2
Snodland 15 E6
Soberton 7 G4
Soham 14 D1
Sole Street 55 H5
Solihull 13 E1
Solihull 57 E5
Solihull Lodge 56 D5
Sollas (Solas) 44 B6
Sollom 58 C1
Solva 10 A3
Somercotes 19 E2
Somerford 56 C2
Somersham 14 C1
Somerton 6 A3
Sonning Common 13 H5
Soughton 22 B6
Soughton 58 A6
South Acton 54 C4
South Anston 24 C5
South Ascot 54 A5
South Benfleet 15 E5
South Brent 4 D5
South Cave 25 E3
South Cerney 12 D5
South Croydon 55 E5
South Darenth 14 D6
South Darenth 55 G4
South Dell
  (Dail Bho Dheas) 44 E1
South Elmsall 24 B4

South Green 55 H2
South Harefield 54 B3
South Hayling 7 H5
South Heath 54 A1
South Hetton 29 E3
South Hornchurch 55 G3
South Killingholme 25 F4
South Kirkby 24 B4
South Littleton 12 D2
South Mimms 54 D1
South Molton 5 E2
South Normanton 19 E2
South Norwood 55 E5
South Ockendon 14 D5
South Ockendon 55 G3
South Oxhey 54 C2
South Petherton 6 A4
South Queensferry 32 D2
South Ruislip 54 C3
South Shields 29 E2
**South Street
  Gt.Lon. 55 F6**
**South Street
  Kent 55 H5**
South Tottenham 55 E3
South Weald 55 G2
South Wingfield 19 E2
South Wonston 7 F3
South Woodham
  Ferrers 15 E5
South Yardley 57 E4
Southall 54 C3
Southam 13 F1
Southam 57 H6
Southampton 7 F4
**Southborough
  Gt.Lon. 55 F5**
Southborough Kent 8 D3
Southbourne 7 H4
Southdene 58 C3
Southend 30 C6
Southend-on-Sea 15 E5
Southery 20 C5
Southfields 54 D4
Southfleet 14 D6
Southfleet 55 H4
Southgate 11 E5
Southgate 55 E2
Southminster 15 F5
Southport 22 C4
Southport 58 B1
Southwater 8 B4
Southwell 19 G2
Southwick W.Suss. 8 B5
Southwick Wilts. 6 C2
Southwold 21 H6
Sowerby 29 E6
Sowerby Bridge 23 F3
Spalding 20 A3
Sparkhill 56 D4
Spean Bridge (Drochaid an
  Aonachain) 39 F6
Speen 13 H4
Speke 56 C4
Speldhurst 8 D3
Spen Green 59 G6
Spencers Wood 13 H6
Spennymoor 28 D4
Spernall 56 D6
Spey Bay 40 D2
Spilsby 25 G5
Spinningdale 39 H1
Spital 54 A4
Spitalbrook 55 E1
Spittalfield 36 D2
Spixworth 21 F4
Spofforth 24 B2
Spratton 13 H1
Spring Grove 54 C4
Springfield 37 E4
Springfield 56 D4
**Springhill
  (Great Wyrley) 56 C2**
**Springhill
  (Hammerwich) 56 D2**
Springside 31 G5
Springwell 28 D3
Sproatley 25 F3
Sproston Green 59 F6
Sprotbrough 24 C4

Sproughton 15 G2
Stableford 56 A3
Staffin 38 B2
Stafford 18 C3
Stainburn 27 F4
Staincross 24 B4
Staindrop 28 D4
Staines-upon-Thames
  14 A6
**Staines-upon-Thames
  54 B4**
Stainforth 24 C4
Stalbridge 6 C4
Stalham 21 G3
Stalybridge 23 F5
Stalybridge 59 H3
Stamford 19 H4
Stamford Bridge 24 D2
Stamford Bridge 58 C6
Stamfordham 28 C2
Standeford 56 C2
Standish 22 D4
Standish 58 D1
Standlake 13 F4
Standon 14 C3
Stanford Bridge 56 A6
Stanford Rivers 55 G1
Stanford in the Vale 13 F5
Stanford on Teme 56 A6
Stanford-le-Hope 14 D5
Stanford-le-Hope 55 H3
Stanhope 28 C4
Stanklyn 56 B5
Stanley Dur. 28 D3
Stanley P. & K. 36 D3
Stanley W.Yorks. 24 B3
Stanley Gate 58 C2
**Stanlow
  Ches.W. & C. 58 C5**
Stanlow Shrop. 56 A3
Stanmore 54 C2
Stannington 28 D2
Stansted 55 H5
Stansted
  Mountfitchet 14 D3
Stanton Derbys. 57 F1
Stanton Suff. 15 F1
**Stanton under
  Bardon 57 H1**
Stanway 15 F3
Stanwell 54 B4
Stanwell Moor 54 B4
Stanwick 14 A1
Stapleford 19 E3
Stapleford Abbotts 55 F2
Stapleford Tawney 55 G2
Staplehurst 9 E3
Stapleton 57 H3
Starcross 5 F4
Stareton 57 G5
Starling 59 F1
Startforth 28 C5
Statham 59 E4
Station Town 29 E4
Staveley Cumb. 27 H6
Staveley Derbys. 24 B6
Staxigoe 43 H3
Stebbing 14 D3
Stechford 57 E4
Steeple Ashton 6 D2
Steeple Claydon 13 G3
Steeple Morden 14 B2
Steeton 23 F2
Stenalees 3 H4
Stenhousemuir 32 A1
Stepney 55 E3
Stepps 31 H3
Stevenage 14 B3
Stevenston 31 F4
Steventon 13 F5
Stewarton 31 G4
Stewkley 13 H3
Steyning 8 B5
Stilton 20 A5
Stirchley Tel. & W. 56 A2
Stirchley W.Mid. 56 D4
Stirling (Sruighlea) 32 A1
Stithians 3 G5
Stivichall 57 G5
Stoak 58 C5

Stock 55 H2
Stockingford 57 G3
Stockport 23 E5
Stockport 59 G3
Stocksbridge 24 A5
Stockton *Shrop.* 56 A3
Stockton *Tel. & W.* 56 A1
Stockton *Warks.* 57 H6
Stockton Heath 59 E4
Stockton on Teme 56 A6
Stockton-on-Tees 29 E4
Stoer 42 A4
Stogursey 5 G1
Stoke 15 E6
Stoke 57 G5
Stoke D'Abernon 54 C6
Stoke Gabriel 5 E6
Stoke Golding 57 G3
Stoke Green 54 A3
Stoke Heath 56 C6
Stoke Holy Cross 21 F4
Stoke Mandeville 13 H4
Stoke Newington 55 E3
Stoke Poges 14 A5
Stoke Poges 54 A3
Stoke Pound 56 C6
Stoke Prior 12 D1
Stoke Prior 56 C6
Stoke St. Gregory 6 A3
Stoke sub Hamdon 6 A4
Stoke-on-Trent 18 B2
Stokenchurch 13 H5
Stokenham 5 E6
Stokesley 29 F5
Stondon Massey 55 G1
Stone *Bucks.* 13 H4
Stone *Kent* 14 D6
Stone *Kent* 55 G4
Stone *Staffs.* 18 C3
Stone *Worcs.* 56 B5
Stone Street 55 G6
Stonebridge 57 F4
Stonehaven 41 F6
Stonehill 54 A5
Stonehouse
  Ches.W. & C. 58 D5
Stonehouse *Glos.* 12 C4
Stonehouse *S.Lan.* 32 A3
Stoneleigh *Surr.* 54 D5
Stoneleigh *Warks.* 13 F1
Stoneleigh *Warks.* 57 G5
Stonesfield 13 F4
Stoney Stanton 19 E5
Stoney Stanton 57 H3
Stoneyburn 32 B2
Stoneywood 41 F5
Stonnall 56 D2
Storeton 58 B4
Stornoway
  (Steòrnabhagh) 44 E3
Storrington 8 A5
Stotfold 14 B3
Stoughton 54 A6
Stourbridge 18 B5
Stourbridge 56 B4
Stourport-on-Severn 12 C1
Stourport-on-Severn
  56 B5
Stourton 56 B4
Stow-on-the-Wold 13 E3
Stowe 57 E1
Stowmarket 15 F2
Stowupland 15 F2
Strachan 41 E6
Strachur
  (Clachan Strachur) 31 F1
Stradbroke 15 G1
Stranraer 26 A2
Stratfield Mortimer 13 G6
Stratford 55 E3
Stratford-upon-Avon 13 E2
Strathaven 32 A3
Strathblane 31 H3
Strathdon 40 D5
Strathpeffer (Strath
  Pheofhair) 39 G3
Strathtay 36 C2
Strathy 43 E2
Strathyre 31 H1
Stratton *Cornw.* 4 B3

Stratton *Glos.* 12 D4
Strawberry Hill 54 C4
Streatham 54 D4
Streatham Vale 54 D4
Street 6 A3
Street Ashton 57 H4
Streethay 57 E1
Streetly 56 D3
Strensall 24 C1
Stretford 23 E5
Stretford 59 F3
Stretham 14 D1
Stretton 59 E4
Stretton
  (Penkridge) 56 B1
Stretton en le Field 57 G1
Stretton under
  Fosse 57 H4
Stretton-on-Dunsmore
  13 F1
Stretton-on-Dunsmore
  57 H5
Strichen 41 G3
Strines 59 H4
Stromness 45 B3
Strone 31 F2
Stronmilchan (Sròn nam
  Mialchon) 35 G3
Strontian
  (Sròn an t-Sithein) 35 E1
Strood 15 E6
Stroud 12 C4
Stroude 54 B5
Stryt-cae-rhedyn 58 A6
Stuartfield 41 G3
Stubber's Green 56 D2
Stubbington 7 G4
Stubbins 59 F1
Stubshaw Cross 58 D2
Studley 12 D1
Studley 56 D6
Studley Common 56 D6
Sturminster Marshall 6 D4
Sturminster Newton 6 C4
Sturry 15 G6
Sturton by Stow 24 D5
Styal 59 G4
Sudbrooke 25 E6
Sudbury *Gt.Lon.* 54 C3
Sudbury *Suff.* 15 E2
Sudden 59 G1
Sulhamstead 13 G6
Summerfield 56 B5
Summit 59 H1
Sun Green 59 H3
Sunbury-on-Thames
  14 B6
Sunbury-on-Thames
  54 C5
Sunderland 29 E3
Sundridge 55 F6
Sunningdale 14 A6
Sunningdale 54 A5
Sunninghill 14 A6
Sunninghill 54 A5
Sunniside 28 D3
Surbiton 54 C5
Sutterton 20 A3
Sutton *Cambs.* 14 C1
Sutton *Gt.Lon.* 14 B6
Sutton *Gt.Lon.* 54 D5
Sutton *Shrop.* 56 A4
Sutton *Suff.* 15 H2
Sutton Bridge 20 B3
Sutton Cheney 57 H2
Sutton Coldfield 18 D5
Sutton Coldfield 57 E3
Sutton Courtenay 13 G5
Sutton Green 54 B6
Sutton Lane Ends 59 H5
Sutton Leach 58 D3
Sutton Maddock 56 A2
Sutton Valence 9 E3
Sutton Weaver 58 D5
Sutton at Hone 14 D6
Sutton at Hone 55 G4
Sutton in Ashfield 19 E2
Sutton on Sea 25 H5
Sutton on Trent 24 D6
Sutton-in-Craven 23 F2

Swadlincote 19 E4
Swadlincote 57 G1
Swaffham 20 D4
Swallows Cross 55 H2
Swan Green 59 F5
Swanage 6 D6
Swancote 56 A3
Swanland 25 E3
Swanley 14 D6
Swanley 55 G5
Swanley Village 55 G5
Swanmore 7 G4
Swannington 57 H1
Swanscombe 14 D6
Swanscombe 55 H4
Swansea (Abertawe) 11 E5
Swanton Morley 21 E4
Swavesey 14 C1
Sway 7 E5
Swepstone 57 G1
Swettenham 59 G6
Swillington 24 B3
Swindon *Staffs.* 56 B3
Swindon *Swin.* 13 E5
Swindon Village 12 D3
Swineshead 20 A2
Swinton *Gt.Man.* 23 E4
Swinton *Gt.Man.* 59 F2
Swinton *S.Yorks.* 24 B5
Sworton Heath 59 E4
Sydenham 55 E4
Symbister 45 J3
Symington 31 G5
Syston 19 F4
Sytchampton 56 B6

T

Tableyhill 59 F5
Tachbrook Mallory 57 G6
Tadcaster 24 B2
Tadley 13 G6
Tadworth 8 B3
Tadworth 54 D6
Taff's Well
  (Ffynnon Taf) 11 H5
Tain 40 A1
Takeley 14 D3
Talgarth 11 H3
Talmine 42 D2
Tamworth 18 D4
Tamworth 57 F2
Tandridge 55 E6
Tangmere 8 A5
Tannadice 37 E2
Tansley 19 E2
Tanworth in Arden 57 E5
Taplow 54 A3
Tarbert (Jura)
  Arg. & B. 30 C2
Tarbert (Loch Fyne)
  Arg. & B. 30 D3
Tarbert *Na H-E.Siar* 44 D4
Tarbet (An Tairbeart) 31 G1
Tarbock Green 58 C4
Tarbolton 31 G5
Tardebigge 56 C6
Tarfside 37 E1
Tarland 40 D5
Tarleton 22 C3
Tarlscough 58 C1
Tarporley 22 D6
Tarves 41 F4
Tarvin 22 C6
Tarvin 58 C6
Tarvin Sands 58 C6
Tatsfield 55 F6
Tattenhall 17 G3
Tattershall 20 A2
Tatworth 6 A4
Taunton 5 G2
Taverham 21 F4
Tavistock 4 C3
Tayinloan 30 C4
Tayport 37 E3
Tayvallich 30 D2
Teangue 38 C5

Tedburn St. Mary 5 E4
Teddington 54 C4
Teignmouth 5 F5
Telford 18 A4
Temple Balsall 57 F5
Temple Cloud 6 B2
Tenbury Wells 12 B1
Tenby (Dinbych-y-pysgod)
  10 C4
Tenterden 9 E4
Terrington
  St. Clement 20 C3
Terrington St. John 20 C4
Terry's Green 57 E5
Tetbury 12 C5
Tetney 25 G4
Tettenhall 56 B2
Tettenhall Wood 56 B3
Teviothead 32 D5
Tewkesbury 12 C3
Teynham 15 F6
Thakeham 8 B5
Thame 13 H4
Thames Ditton 54 C5
Thamesmead 55 F3
Thatcham 13 G6
Thatto Heath 58 D3
Thaxted 14 D3
The Bratch 56 B3
The Burf 56 B6
The Delves 56 D3
The Green 58 A6
The Hermitage 54 D6
The Sale 57 E1
The Swillett 54 B2
The Wyke 56 A2
Theale 13 G6
Thelwall 59 E4
Thetford 20 D5
Theydon Bois 14 C5
Theydon Bois 55 F2
Theydon Garnon 55 F2
Theydon Mount 55 F2
Thirsk 29 E5
Thong 55 H4
Thornaby-on-Tees 29 E5
Thornbury 12 B5
Thorne 24 C4
Thorner 24 B3
Thorney *Bucks.* 54 B4
Thorney *Peter.* 20 A4
Thorngumbald 25 F3
Thornhill *D. & G.* 27 E1
Thornhill *Stir.* 31 H1
Thornley 29 E4
Thorns Green 59 F4
Thornton *Fife* 32 C1
Thornton *Lancs.* 22 C2
Thornton *Leics.* 57 H2
Thornton *Mersey.* 58 B2
Thornton Heath 55 E5
Thornton Hough 58 B4
Thornton-le-Dale 29 G6
Thornton-le-Moors 58 C5
Thornwood 55 F1
Thorpe 54 B5
Thorpe Constantine 57 F2
Thorpe Hesley 24 B5
Thorpe Willoughby 24 C3
Thorpe-le-Soken 15 G3
Thorrington 15 F4
Thrapston 14 A1
Three Legged Cross 6 D4
Thringstone 57 H1
Thropton 33 G5
Thrumster 43 H3
Thrupp 12 C4
Thrybergh 24 B5
Thundersley 15 E5
Thurcaston 19 F4
Thurcroft 24 C5
Thurgoland 24 A4
Thurlaston 57 H6
Thurlby 20 A4
Thurnby 19 F4
Thurnscoe 24 B4
Thursby 27 H3
Thurso
  (Inbhir Theòrsa) 43 G2
Thurstaston 58 A4

Thurston 15 F1
Thurston Clough 59 H2
Tibshelf 24 B6
Ticehurst 8 D4
Tickhill 24 C5
Tidbury Green 57 E5
Tidenham 12 B5
Tideswell 24 A6
Tidworth 7 E2
Tilbury 14 D6
Tilbury 55 H4
Tile Hill 57 F5
Tillicoultry 32 B1
Tillyfourie 41 E5
Tilney St. Lawrence 20 C4
Tilstone Fearnall 58 D6
Timbersbrook 59 G6
Timperley 59 F4
Timsbury 6 B2
Timsgearraidh 44 C3
Tintagel 3 H2
Tipton 56 C3
Tiptree 15 E4
Tisbury 6 D3
Titsey 55 F6
Tiverton
  Ches.W. & C. 58 D6
Tiverton *Devon* 5 F3
Tobermory 34 D2
Tockwith 24 B2
Toddington 14 A3
Todmorden 23 F3
Tolastadh
  a' Chaolais 44 D3
Tollesbury 15 F4
Tolworth 54 C5
Tomatin 40 A4
Tomintoul 40 C5
Tomnavoulin 40 C4
Tonbridge 8 D3
Tondu 11 F5
Tong 56 A2
Tong Norton 56 A2
Tongham 7 H2
Tongue 42 D3
Tonna 11 F5
Tonypandy 11 G5
Tonyrefail 11 G5
Toot Hill 55 G1
Tooting Graveney 54 D4
Top of Hebers 59 G2
Topcliffe 24 B1
Toppings 59 F1
Topsham 5 F4
Torphins 41 E5
Torpoint 4 C6
Torquay 5 F5
Torrance 31 H3
Torridon 39 E3
Torton 56 B5
Torver 27 G6
Totaig 38 A3
Totland 7 F5
Totnes 5 E5
Tottenham 55 E2
Totteridge 54 D2
Tottington 23 E4
Tottington 59 F1
Totton 7 F4
Tow Law 28 D4
Towcester 13 G2
Town End 58 C4
Town Green 58 C2
Town Yetholm 33 F4
Town of Lowton 59 E3
Towns Green 59 E6
Towyn 22 A6
Toy's Hill 55 F6
Trafford Centre 59 F3
Trafford Park 59 F3
Tranent 32 D2
Tranmere 58 B4
Trap Street 59 G6
Trap's Green 57 E6
Trawden 23 F3
Trawsfynydd 16 D4
Tredegar 11 H4
Tredington 13 E2
Treeton 24 B5
Trefeglwys 17 E6

Trefnant 22 A6
Tregaron 11 E2
Tregynon 17 E6
Treharris 11 G5
Treherbert 11 G5
Tremadog 16 C3
Treorchy 11 G5
Trescott 56 B3
Tresta 45 H4
Treuddyn 17 F3
Trimdon 29 E4
Trimley St. Martin 15 G3
Trimley St. Mary 15 G3
Trimpley 56 A5
Trimsaran 10 D4
Tring 14 A4
Troedyrhiw 11 G4
Troon *Cornw.* 3 F5
Troon *S.Ayr.* 31 G5
Trottiscliffe 15 H5
Trowbridge 6 C2
Trull 5 G2
Trumps Green 54 A5
Truro 3 G4
Trysull 56 B3
Tuckhill 56 A4
Tullibody 32 A1
Tullynessle 41 E5
Tulse Hill 55 E4
Tumble (Y Tymbl) 11 E4
Tunga 44 E3
Turn 59 G1
Turner's Green 57 E6
Turnford 55 E1
Turriff 41 F3
Turton Bottoms 59 F1
Turvey 14 A2
Tutbury 18 D3
Tutnall 56 C5
Tutshill 12 B5
Tuxford 24 D6
Twatt 45 H4
Twemlow Green 59 F6
Twickenham 54 C4
Twiss Green 59 E3
Twitton 55 G6
Two Gates 57 F2
Two Mills 58 B5
Twycross 57 G2
Twyford *Hants.* 7 F3
Twyford *W'ham* 13 H6
Twyning 12 C3
Tye Common 55 H2
Tye Green 55 F1
Tyldesley 22 D4
Tyldesley 59 E2
Tyler's Green 55 G1
Tylers Green 14 A5
Tylers Green 54 A2
Tylorstown 11 G5
Tyndrum
  (Taigh an Droma) 35 H3
Tynemouth 29 E2
Tyseley 57 E4
Tytherington 59 H5
Tywardreath 3 H4
Tywyn 16 C5

U

Uckfield 8 C4
Uddingston 31 H3
Udny Green 41 F4
Udny Station 41 G4
Uffculme 5 F3
Ufton 57 G6
Ugborough 4 D6
Uig (Uige) 38 B2
Ulbster 43 H3
Ulceby 25 F4
Uley 12 C5
Ulgham 28 D1
Ullapool (Ullapul) 39 F1
Ullenhall 57 E6
Ulverston 22 B1
Underriver 55 G6
Underwood *Newport* 12 A5
Underwood *Notts.* 19 E2

Undy 12 A5
Unsworth 59 G2
Up Holland 58 D2
Upavon 7 E2
Upchurch 15 E6
Uphampton 56 B6
Uplyme 6 A5
Upminster 55 G3
Upper Arley 56 A4
Upper Aston 56 B3
Upper Basildon 13 G6
Upper Bayble (Pabail Uarach)
  44 F3
Upper Beeding 8 B5
Upper Bentley 56 C6
Upper Catshill 56 C5
Upper Clatford 7 F2
Upper Dallachy 40 D2
**Upper Eastern
  Green 57 F4**
Upper Gornal 56 C3
Upper Halliford 54 B5
Upper Halling 55 H5
Upper Heyford 13 F3
Upper Killay 11 E5
Upper Largo 37 E4
Upper Longdon 56 C2
Upper Ludstone 56 B3
Upper Lydbrook 12 B4
Upper Norwood 55 E4
Upper Poppleton 24 C2
Upper Rissington 13 E3
Upper Shuckburgh 57 H6
Upper Tean 18 C3
Upper Tooting 54 D4
Upper Witton 56 D3
Uppermill 23 F4
Uppingham 19 G5
Uppermill 59 H2
Upshire 55 F1
Upton *Ches.W. & C.* 58 C6
Upton *Leics.* 57 G3
Upton *Mersey.* 58 A4
Upton *Slo.* 54 A4
Upton Park 55 F3
Upton St. Leonards 12 C4
Upton Warren 56 C6
Upton upon Severn 12 C2
Upwell 20 C4
Urmston 23 E5
Urmston 59 F3
Urquhart 40 C2
Ushaw Moor 28 D3
Usk (Brynbuga) 12 A4
Uttoxeter 18 C3
Uxbridge 14 A5
Uxbridge 54 B3
Uyeasound 45 J1

V

Valley (Y Fali) 16 A2
Valleyfield 32 B1
Veensgarth 45 H4
Ventnor 7 G6
Verwood 6 D4
Vidlin 45 H3
Vigo 56 D2
Vigo Village 55 H5
Virginia Water 14 A6
Virginia Water 54 A5
Voe 45 H3

W

Waddesdon 13 H4
Waddicar 58 B3
Waddington 25 E6
Waddon 55 E5
Wadebridge 3 H3
Wadhurst 8 D4
Wainfleet All Saints 20 B2
Wakefield 24 B3
Walberton 8 A5
Wales 24 B5
Walkden 23 E4
Walkden 59 F2
Walkington 25 E3
Walkwood 56 D6

Wall 57 E2
Wall Heath 56 B4
Wallasey 22 B5
Wallasey 58 A3
Wallingford 13 G5
Wallington 54 D5
Walls 45 G4
Wallsend 29 E2
Walmersley 59 G1
Walmley 57 E3
Walpole St. Peter 20 C4
Walsall 18 C5
Walsall 56 D3
Walsall Wood 56 D2
Walsgrave on Sowe 57 G4
Walter's Ash 13 H5
Waltham Abbey 14 C4
Waltham Abbey 55 E1
Waltham Chase 7 G4
Waltham Cross 55 E1
Walthamstow 14 C5
Walthamstow 55 E3
Walton 24 B4
Walton 58 B3
Walton on the Hill 54 D6
Walton on the Naze 15 G3
Walton-on-Thames 14 B6
Walton-on-Thames 54 B6
Walton-on-Trent 57 F1
Walwen 58 A5
Wanborough 13 E5
Wandsworth 14 B6
Wandsworth 54 D4
Wantage 13 F5
Wappenbury 57 G6
Warborough 13 G5
Warboys 14 C1
Warburton 59 E4
Ward End 57 E4
Warden 15 F6
Wardle 23 F4
Wardle 59 H1
Wardley 59 F2
Wardsend 59 H4
Ware 14 C4
Wareham 6 D5
Waresley 56 B5
Wargrave *Mersey.* 58 D3
Wargrave *W'ham* 13 H6
Warkworth 33 H5
Warley *Essex* 55 G2
Warley *W.Mid.* 56 D4
Warlingham 8 C3
Warlingham 55 E6
Warmingham 59 F6
Warminster 6 C2
Warners End 54 B1
Warnham 8 B4
Warren 59 G5
Warrington 22 D5
Warrington 59 E4
Warsash 7 F4
Warton *Lancs.* 22 D1
Warton *Warks.* 57 F2
Warwick 13 E1
Warwick 57 F6
Warwick Wold 55 E6
Washford 56 D6
Washingborough 25 E6
Washington *T. & W.* 29 E3
Washington *W.Suss.* 8 B5
Watchet 5 F1
Water End 54 D1
Water Orton 18 D5
Water Orton 57 E3
Waterbeach 14 C1
Waterfoot 31 H4
Wateringbury 8 D3
Wateringbury 55 H6
Waterloo *Gt.Man.* 59 H2
Waterloo *Mersey.* 58 B3
Waterlooville 7 G4
Watersheddings 59 H2
Waterside 54 A1
Watford 14 B5
Watford 54 C2
Wath upon Dearne 24 B4
Watlington *Norf.* 20 C4
Watlington *Oxon.* 13 G5
Watten 43 H3

Wattisham 15 F2
Watton 21 E4
Watton at Stone 14 C4
Watton's Green 55 G2
Waunfawr 16 C3
Waverton 22 C6
Waverton 58 C6
Wavertree 58 B4
Wawne 25 E3
Wealdstone 54 C2
Weatheroak Hill 56 D5
Weaverham 22 D6
Weaverham 59 E5
Webheath 56 D6
Weddington 57 G3
Wedmore 6 A2
Wednesbury 56 C3
Wednesfield 56 C2
Weedon Bec 13 G2
Weeford 57 E2
Weeley 15 G3
Weem 36 B2
Weeting 20 D5
Weldon 19 H5
Welford-on-Avon 13 E2
Welham Green 54 D1
Well End 54 D2
Well Hill 55 F5
Well Street 55 H6
Wellesbourne 13 E2
Welling 55 F4
Wellingborough 13 H1
Wellingore 19 H2
Wellington 55 G2
Wells 6 B2
Wells Green 57 E4
Wells-next-the-Sea 21 E2
Wellsborough 57 G2
Welshpool
  (Y Trallwng) 17 F5
Welton *E.Riding* 25 E3
Welton *Lincs.* 25 E5
Welwyn 14 B4
Welwyn Garden City 14 B4
Wem 18 A3
Wembdon 5 G2
Wembley 14 B5
Wembley 54 C3
Wembley Park 54 C3
Wembury 4 D6
Wemyss Bay 31 F3
Wendover 13 H4
Wennington 55 G3
Wenvoe 11 H6
Weoley Castle 56 D4
Wepre 58 A6
Wergs 56 B2
Wervin 58 C5
West Acton 54 C3
West Auckland 28 D4
West Ayton 29 H6
West Bergholt 15 F3
West Bridgford 19 F3
West Bromwich 18 C5
West Bromwich 56 D3
West Byfleet 14 A6
West Byfleet 54 A6
West Calder 32 B2
West Chiltington
  Common 8 A5
West Clandon 54 B6
West Coker 6 B4
West Derby 58 B3
West Drayton 54 B4
West End 54 D1
West End (Bisley) 54 A5
West End (Esher) 54 C5
West Green 55 E3
West Hagley 56 C4
West Hallam 19 E2
West Ham 55 E3
West Hanningfield 15 E5
West Harrow 54 C3
**West Heath
  Ches.E. 59 G6**
**West Heath
  Gt.Lon. 55 F4**
West Heath *W.Mid.* 56 D5
West Hendon 54 D3
West Hill 5 F4

West Hoathly 8 C4
West Horndon 55 H3
West Horsley 8 A3
West Horsley 54 B6
West Hyde 54 B2
West Kilbride 31 F4
West Kingsdown 14 D6
West Kingsdown 55 G5
West Kirby 22 B5
West Kirby 58 A4
West Lavington 6 D2
West Linton 32 C3
West Lulworth 6 C5
West Malling 8 D3
West Malling 55 H6
West Mersea 15 F4
West Molesey 54 C5
West Moors 6 D4
West Norwood 55 E4
West Park 58 D3
West Parley 6 D5
West Peckham 55 H6
West Rainton 29 E3
West Sandwick 45 H2
West Thurrock 55 G4
West Tilbury 55 H4
West Walton 20 B4
West Wellow 7 E3
West Wickham 55 E5
West Winch 20 C4
West Wittering 7 H5
West Wycombe 13 H5
Westbourne 7 H4
**Westbourne
  Green 54 D3**
Westbury 6 C2
Westergate 8 A5
Westerham 8 C3
Westerham 55 F6
Westerleigh 12 B6
Westfield 9 E5
Westham 8 D5
Westhead 58 C2
Westhill *Aber.* 41 F5
Westhill *High.* 40 A3
Westhoughton 22 D4
Westhoughton 59 E2
Westhumble 54 C6
Westleigh 59 E2
Westley Heights 55 H3
Westminster 14 B6
Westminster 54 D4
Westmuir 37 E2
Weston *Dorset* 6 B6
Weston *Halton* 58 D4
Weston *Lincs.* 20 A3
Weston Heath 56 A1
Weston Point 58 C4
Weston Rhyn 17 F4
Weston Turville 13 H4
Weston in Arden 57 G4
**Weston under
  Wetherley 57 G6**
Weston-super-Mare 12 A6
**Weston-under-Lizard
  56 B1**
Westoning 14 A3
Westonzoyland 6 A3
Westruther 33 E3
Westvale 58 C3
Westward Ho! 4 C2
Westwood Heath 57 F5
Westwoodside 24 D5
Wetherby 24 B3
Wethersfield 15 E3
Wettenhall 59 E6
Wettenhall Green 59 E6
Wexham Street 54 A3
Weybourne 14 A6
Weybridge 54 B5
Weymouth 6 B6
Whaley Bridge 23 F5
Whalley 23 E3
Whaplode 20 B3
Wharncliffe Side 24 A5
Wharton 59 E6
Whateley 57 F3
Whauphill 26 D3
Wheathampstead 14 B4
Wheatley 13 G4

Wheatley Hill 29 E4
Wheaton Aston 18 B4
Wheaton Aston 56 B1
Wheldrake 24 C2
Whelley 58 D2
Whelpley Hill 54 A1
Whelston 58 A5
Whetstone 54 D2
Whickham 28 D2
Whiddon Down 4 D4
Whimple 5 F4
Whissendine 19 G4
Whisterfield 59 G5
Whiston *Mersey.* **58 C3**
Whiston *Staffs.* **56 B1**
Whiston Cross 56 A2
Whitacre Fields 57 F3
Whitacre Heath 57 F3
Whitburn *T. & W.* 29 E2
Whitburn *W.Loth.* 32 B2
Whitby
    Ches.W. & C. **58 B5**
Whitby *N.Yorks.* 29 G5
Whitbyheath 58 B5
Whitchurch *Hants.* 7 F2
Whitchurch *Shrop.* 18 A2
White Coppice 59 E1
White Waltham 13 H6
Whitefield 23 E4
Whitefield 59 G2
Whitegate 59 E6
Whitehall 45 D2
Whitehaven 27 F5
Whitehill 7 H3
Whitehills 41 E2
Whitehouse
    Common 57 E3
Whiteley 7 G4
Whiteley Green 59 H5
Whiteley Village 54 B5
Whiterashes 41 F4
Whiteshill 12 C4
Whithorn 26 C3
Whiting Bay 31 E5
Whitland
    (Hendy-Gwyn) 10 C4
Whitley 57 G5
Whitley Bay 29 E2
Whitley Row 55 F6
Whitlock's End 57 E5
Whitmore 18 B2
Whitnash 57 G6
Whitstable 15 G6
Whittingham 33 G5
Whittington *Shrop.* 17 G4
Whittington *Staffs.* 18 B5
Whittington
    (Kinver) 56 B4
Whittington
    (Lichfield) 57 E2
Whittle-le-Woods 22 D3
Whittlesey 20 A5
Whittlesford 14 C2
Whittlestone Head 59 F1
Whitton 54 C4
Whitwell 24 C6
Whitwick 57 H1
Whitworth 23 E4
Whitworth 59 G1
Whyteleafe 55 E6
Wibtoft 57 H4
Wichenford 56 A6
Wick 12 C6
Wick (Inbhir Ùige) 43 H3
Wickford 15 E5
Wickham 7 G4
Wickham Bishops 15 E4
Wickham Market 15 G2
Wickwar 12 C5
Widdrington Station 28 D1
Wide Open 28 D2
Widecombe in the
    Moor 5 E5
Widford 55 H1
Widnes 22 D5
Widnes 58 D4
Wigan 22 D4
Wigan 58 D2
Wigginton 57 F2
Wigston 19 F5

Wigston Parva 57 H4
Wigton 27 G3
Wigtown 26 C3
Wilberfoss 24 D2
Wildboarclough 59 H6
Wilden 56 B5
Wildhill 54 D1
Wildmoor 56 C5
Willand 5 F3
Willaston 22 C6
Willaston 58 B5
Willenhall
    (Coventry) 57 G5
Willenhall (Walsall) 56 C3
Willesden 54 D3
Willey 57 H4
Willey Green 54 A6
Willingale 55 G1
Willingham 14 C1
Willington *Derbys.* 18 D3
Willington *Dur.* 28 D4
Willington Corner 58 D6
Williton 5 F1
Willow Green 59 E5
Wilmington 14 D6
Wilmington 55 G4
Wilmslow 23 E5
Wilmslow 59 G4
Wilnecote 57 F2
Wilpshire 22 D3
Wilsden 23 F3
Wilstead 14 A2
Wilton 6 D3
Wimblebury 56 D1
Wimbledon 14 B6
Wimbledon 54 D4
Wimblington 20 B5
Wimborne Minster 6 D4
Wincanton 6 C3
Wincham 59 E5
Winchburgh 32 B2
Winchcombe 12 D3
Winchester 7 F3
Winchmore Hill
    Bucks. **54 A2**
Winchmore Hill
    Gt.Lon. **55 E2**
Wincle 59 H6
Windermere 27 H6
Windle Hill 58 B5
Windlehurst 59 H4
Windlesham 14 A6
Windlesham 54 A5
Windsor 14 A6
Windsor 54 A4
Windygates 37 E4
Winford 12 B6
Wing 13 H3
Wingate 29 E4
Wingates 59 E2
Wingerworth 24 B6
Wingham 9 G3
Winkfield 14 A6
Winkfield 54 A4
Winkleigh 4 D3
Winnersh 13 H6
Winnington 59 E5
Winscombe 6 A2
Winsford 22 D6
Winsford 59 E6
Winsley 12 C6
Winslow 13 H3
Winterbourne 12 B5
Winterslow 7 E3
Winterton 25 E4
Winwick *Cambs.* 20 A5
Winwick *Warr.* 59 E3
Wirksworth 18 D2
Wisbech 20 B4
Wisbech St. Mary 20 B4
Wisborough Green 8 A4
Wishaw *N.Lan.* 32 A3
Wishaw *Warks.* 57 E3
Wisley 54 B6
Wistaston 18 A2
Witchford 14 D1
Witham 15 E4
Witheridge 5 E3
Witherley 57 G3
Withernsea 25 G3

Withington 12 B2
Withington 59 G3
Withington Green 59 G5
Withybrook 57 H4
Witley 8 A4
Witney 13 F4
Wittering 19 H4
Wittersham 9 E4
Witton 56 B6
Witton Gilbert 28 D3
Wiveliscombe 5 F2
Wivelsfield 8 C4
Wivenhoe 15 F3
Woburn Sands 14 A3
Woking 8 A3
Woking 54 B6
Wokingham 13 H6
Woldingham 55 E6
Wollaston
    N.N'hants. 14 A1
Wollaston *W.Mid.* 56 B4
Wollescote 56 C4
Wolsingham 28 C4
Wolston 13 F1
Wolston 57 H5
Wolverhampton 18 C5
Wolverhampton 56 C3
Wolverley 12 C1
Wolverley 56 B5
Wolverton 57 F6
Wolvey 19 E5
Wolvey 57 H4
Wolvey Heath 57 H4
Wombourne 18 B5
Wombourne 56 B3
Wombwell 24 B4
Wonersh 8 A3
Wooburn 54 A3
Wooburn Green 54 A3
Wood Eaton 56 B1
Wood End 56 C2
Wood End
    (Fillongley) 57 F4
Wood End
    (Redditch) 57 E5
Wood End
    (Tamworth) 57 F3
Wood Green *Essex* 55 F1
Wood Green *Gt.Lon.* 14 C5
Wood Green
    Gt.Lon. **55 E2**
Wood Street
    Village 54 A6
Woodbridge 15 G2
Woodbury 5 F4
Woodchurch 9 F4
Woodchurch 58 A4
Woodcote *Oxon.* 13 G5
Woodcote
    Tel. & W. **56 A1**
Woodcote Green 56 C5
Woodford *Gt.Lon.* 55 F2
Woodford *Gt.Man.* 59 G4
Woodford
    N.N'hants. 14 A1
Woodford Bridge 55 F2
Woodford Green 55 F2
Woodgate *W.Mid.* 56 C4
Woodgate *Worcs.* 56 C6
Woodhall Spa 25 F6
Woodham 54 B5
Woodham Ferrers 15 E5
Woodhead 41 H4
Woodhey 58 B4
Woodhill 56 A4
Woodhouse 19 F4
Woodhouse Eaves 19 F4
Woodhouse Green 59 H6
Woodhouses 59 G2
Woodhouses
    (Barton- under-
    Needwood) 57 E1
Woodhouses
    (Burntwood) 56 D2
Woodlands 56 A4
Woodley 59 H3
Woodmancote 12 D3
Woodmansterne 54 D6
Woodside *Brack.F.* 54 A4
Woodside *Gt.Lon.* 55 E5

Woodside *Herts.* 54 D1
Woodside *W.Mid.* 56 C4
Woodstock 13 F4
Woodvale 58 B1
Woodville 19 E4
Woodville 57 G1
Wool 6 C5
Woolacombe 4 C1
Woolavington 6 A2
Wooler 33 G4
Woolfold 59 F1
Woollensbrook 55 E1
Woolmere Green 56 C6
Woolpit 15 F1
Woolscott 57 H6
Woolston 59 E4
Woolton 58 C4
Woolwich 14 C6
Woolwich 55 F4
Wootton *Bed.* 14 A2
Wootton *Oxon.* 13 F4
Wootton Bassett 12 D5
Wootton Bridge 7 G5
Wootton Wawen 57 E6
Worcester 12 C2
Worcester Park 54 D5
Wordsley 56 B4
Worfield 56 A3
Workington 27 F4
Worksop 24 C6
Worlds End 57 E4
Worlingham 21 G5
Wormley 55 E1
Wormley West End 55 E1
Worplesdon 8 A3
Worplesdon 54 A6
Worsbrough 24 B4
Worsley 59 F2
Worthing 8 B5
Worthington 19 E3
Wotton-under-Edge 12 C5
Wragby 25 F6
Wrangle 20 B2
Wraxall 12 A6
Wraysbury 54 B4
Wrexham (Wrecsam) 17 G3
Wribbenhall 56 A5
Wrightington Bar 58 D1
Wrington 12 A6
Writtle 14 D4
Writtle 55 H1
Wrotham 55 H6
Wrotham Heath 55 H6
Wrotham Hill Park 55 H5
Wrottesley 56 B2
Wroughton 13 E5
Wroxall 7 G6
Wroxall 57 F5
Wroxham 21 G4
Wyberton 20 B2
Wychbold 56 C6
Wychnor 57 E1
Wychnor Bridges 57 E1
Wye 9 F3
Wyke 54 A6
Wyken *Shrop.* 56 A3
Wyken *W.Mid.* 57 G4
Wylde Green 57 E3
Wymondham 21 F4
Wythall 12 D1
Wythall 56 D5
Wythenshawe 59 G4
Wyton 14 B1

Y

Y Felinheli 16 C2
Yapton 8 A5
Yardley 57 E4
Yardley Gobion 13 H2
Yarm 29 E5
Yarmouth 7 F5
Yarnton 13 F4
Yate 12 C5
Yatehouse Green 59 F6
Yateley 13 H6
Yatton 12 A6
Yaxley 20 A5
Yeading 54 C3
Yeadon 24 A2

Yealmpton 4 D6
Yelverton 4 D5
Yeovil 6 B4
Yeovilton 6 B3
Yew Green 57 F6
Ynys-ddu 11 H5
York 24 C2
Yorkley 12 B4
Youlgreave 24 A6
Yoxall 18 D4
Yoxall 57 E1
Ysbyty Ystwyth 11 F1
Ystalyfera 11 F4
Ystrad 11 G5
Ystrad Mynach 11 H5
Ystradgynlais 11 F4
Ythanwells 41 E4

Abbreviations

Banbr.	Banbridge	*N.Down*	North Down	*S.Dub.*	South Dublin	*Wexf.*	Wexford
Kilk.	Kilkenny	*N.Tipp*	North Tipperary	*Water.*	Waterford		

A

Aasleagh 48 C4
Abbeyfeale 50 C3
Abbeyleix 49 G6
Adare 50 D2
Ailt an Chorráin
  (Burtonport) 46 B2
An Baile Breac
  (Ballybrack) 50 A5
An Clochán Liath
  (Dungloe) 46 B2
An Mhala Raithní
  (Mulrany) 48 B3
An Spidéal (Spiddal) 48 C5
Annahilt 47 G4
Annalong 47 G5
Antrim 47 G3
Ardara 46 B3
Ardee 47 F6
Ardglass 47 H4
Arklow 52 C4
Armagh 47 F4
Armoy 47 F1
Arvagh 49 G3
Ashbourne 52 B1
Athboy 52 A1
Athenry 48 D5
Athleague 49 F4
Athlone 49 F4
Athy 52 A3
Augher 47 E4
Aughnacloy 47 E4
Aughrim 52 C3
Avoca 52 C3

B

Bagenalstown 52 A4
Baile Chláir
  (Claregalway) 48 D5
Baile Mhic Íre
  (Ballymakeery) 50 D5
Baile na Finne
  (Fintown) 46 C2
Bailieborough 47 E6
Balbriggan 52 C1
Ballaghaderreen 49 E3
Ballina 48 D2
Ballinafad 46 B5
Ballinalack 49 G4
Ballinamallard 46 D4
Ballinamore 46 C5
Ballinasloe 49 F5
Ballindine 48 D4
Ballinrobe 48 D4
Ballon 52 B4
Ballybay 47 E5
Ballybofey 46 C3
Ballybunion 50 B3
Ballycanew 52 C4
Ballycastle *Mayo* 48 C1
Ballycastle *Moyle* 47 G1
Ballyclare 47 G3
Ballyconnell 46 D5
Ballycroy 48 B2
Ballydesmond 50 C4
Ballygar 49 E4
Ballygawley 47 E4
Ballygorman 46 D1
Ballyhale 52 A5
Ballyhaunis 48 D3
Ballyheige 50 B3
Ballyjamesduff 47 E6
Ballykelly 47 E2
Ballylynan 52 A3
Ballymacarberry 51 G3
Ballymacmague 51 G4
Ballymacoda 51 F5
Ballymahon 49 G4
Ballymena 47 F2
Ballymoney 47 F2
Ballymote 46 B5
Ballymurphy 52 A4

Ballynahinch 47 G4
Ballyragget 51 G2
Ballyshannon 46 C4
Ballyvaughan 48 D5
Ballyward 47 G4
Baltinglass 52 B3
Banagher 49 F5
Banbridge 47 G4
Bandon 50 D5
Bangor *Mayo* 48 B2
Bangor *N.Down* 47 H3
Banteer 50 D4
Bantry 50 C5
Béal an Mhuirthead
  (Belmullet) 48 B2
Béal Deirg
  (Belderg) 48 C1
Belcoo 46 C4
Belfast 47 G3
Belfast International
  Airport 47 G3
Belturbet 46 D5
Beragh 47 E3
Bessbrook 47 F5
Bettystown 47 G6
Birr 49 F6
Blackrock 47 F5
Blackwater 52 C5
Blarney 51 E5
Blessington 52 B2
Bohola 48 D3
Borris 52 A4
Borrisokane 49 F6
Borrisoleigh 51 F2
Boyle 46 B5
Bray 52 C2
Broadford 50 D3
Broughshane 47 G2
Bunbeg 46 B2
Bunclody 52 B4
Buncrana 46 D1
Bundoran 46 B4
Bushmills 47 F1
Butlers Bridge 46 D5
Buttevant 51 E4

C

Cahermore 50 B6
Cahir 51 F3
Cahirsiveen 50 A4
Callan 51 G2
Cappoquin 51 F4
Carlingford 47 G5
Carlow 52 A3
Carndonagh 47 E1
Carnlough 47 G2
Carrickfergus 47 G3
Carrickmacross 47 F5
Carrick-on-Shannon 49 F3
Carrick-on-Suir 51 G3
Carrigallen 46 D5
Carrigtohill 51 E5
Carrowdore 47 H3
Carrowkeel 47 E1
Cashel 51 F3
Castlebar 48 C3
Castlebellingham 47 F6
Castleblayney 47 F5
Castlebridge 52 B5
Castlecomer 52 A4
Castleconnell 51 E2
Castlederg 46 D3
Castledermot 52 A3
Castlegregory 50 B3
Castleisland 50 C4
Castlemaine 50 B4
Castlemartyr 51 F5
Castlepollard 49 G4
Castlerea 49 E3
Castletown 49 G6
Castletownbere 50 B6
Cathair Dónall
  (Catherdaniel) 50 A5

Cavan 46 D5
Celbridge 52 B2
Charlestown 48 D3
Charleville 51 E3
Cheekpoint 52 A5
City of Derry Airport 47 E2
Clady 46 D3
Clane 52 B2
Clara 49 G5
Clarecastle 50 D2
Claremorris 48 D3
Clashmore 51 F4
Claudy 47 E2
Clifden 48 B4
Cliffoney 46 B4
Cloghan 49 F5
Clogheen 51 F3
Clonakilty 50 D6
Clonbern 49 E4
Clones 47 E5
Clonmel 51 G3
Clonroche 52 B5
Clonygowan 52 A2
Cloonbannin 50 D4
Clooneagh 49 F3
Coalisland 47 F3
Cobh 51 E5
Coleraine 47 F1
Collooney 46 B5
Comber 47 H3
Cong 48 C4
Connemara Airport 48 C5
Cookstown 47 F3
Cootehill 47 E5
Cork 51 E5
Cork International
  Airport 51 E5
Corofin 48 D6
Courtmacsherry 51 E6
Courtown 52 C4
Craanford 52 B4
Craigavon 47 F4
Creeslough 46 C1
Cregganbaun 48 B3
Crookhaven 50 B6
Croom 51 E3
Crossgar 47 H4
Crosshaven 51 E5
Crossmaglen 47 F5
Crumlin 47 G3
Crusheen 48 D6
Cullybackey 47 F2
Cushendall 47 G2
Cushendun 47 G1

D

Daingean Uí Chúis
  (Dingle) 50 A4
Delvin 52 A1
Derry
  (Londonderry) 46 D2
Donaghadee 47 H3
Donaghmore 47 E4
Donegal 46 C3
Donegal International
  Airport 46 B2
Donoughmore 50 D4
Dooagh 48 B2
Downpatrick 47 H4
Draperstown 47 E3
Drimoleague 50 C6
Drogheda 47 F6
Dromod 49 F3
Dromore *Banbr.* 47 G4
Dromore *Omagh* 46 D4
Dromore West 48 D2
Drumfree 46 D1
Drumkeeran 46 C5
Drummin 52 A5
Dublin 52 C2
Dublin Airport 52 C1
Dún Chaoin
  (Dunquin) 50 A4

Dún Laoghaire 52 C2
Dunboyne 52 B1
Duncannon 52 A6
Duncormick 52 B6
Dundalk 47 F5
Dundonald 47 G3
Dundrum 47 G4
Dungannon 47 F4
Dungarvan *Kilk.* 52 A4
Dungarvan *Water.* 51 G4
Dungiven 47 E2
Dunlavin 52 B3
Dunleer 47 F6
Dunloy 47 F2
Dunmanway 50 D5
Dunmore 49 E4
Dunmore East 52 A6
Durrow 49 G6

E

Edenderry 52 A2
Edgeworthstown 49 G3
Eglinton 47 E2
Ennis 48 D6
Enniscorthy 52 B5
Enniskean 50 D5
Enniskerry 52 C2
Enniskillen 46 D4
Ennistymon 48 C6

F

Farranfore 50 C4
Fermoy 51 E4
Ferns 52 B4
Fethard 51 G3
Fintona 46 D4
Fivemiletown 46 D4
Foxford 48 D2
Foynes 50 D2
Frenchpark 49 E3
Freshford 51 G2

G

Galbally 51 E3
Galway 48 D5
Galway Airport 48 D5
Gaoth Dobhair
  (Gweedore) 46 C2
Garvagh 47 F2
George Best Belfast City
  Airport 47 G3
Glengarriff 50 C5
Glengavlen 46 C5
Glennamaddy 49 E4
Glenties 46 B3
Gob an Choire
  (Achill Sound) 48 B3
Gorey 52 C4
Gort 48 D6
Gort an Choirce
  (Gortahork) 46 C1
Graigue 52 A3
Graiguenamanagh 52 A4
Granard 49 G3
Grange 51 G4
Greenore 47 G5
Greystones 52 C2

H

Halfway 51 E5
Headford 48 D4
Holycross 51 F2
Horseleap 49 E4
Hospital 51 E3
Howth 52 C1
Hurler's Cross 50 D2

I

Inch *Kerry* 50 B4

Inch *Wexf.* 52 C4
Ireland West
  Airport Knock 48 D3
Irvinestown 46 D4

J

Johnstown 51 G2

K

Kanturk 50 D4
Keady 47 F5
Kells *Kilk.* 52 A4
Kells *Meath* 47 E6
Kenmare 50 C5
Kerry Airport 50 C4
Kilbeggan 49 G5
Kilcolgan 48 D5
Kilcommon 51 F3
Kilcoole 52 C2
Kilcormac 49 G5
Kilcullen 52 B2
Kildare 52 A2
Kilkee 50 C2
Kilkeel 47 G5
Kilkenny 52 A4
Killala 48 D2
Killaloe 51 E2
Killarney 50 C4
Killenaule 51 G2
Killimor 49 E5
Killinchy 47 H4
Killinick 52 B5
Killorglin 50 B4
Killurin 52 B5
Killybegs 46 B3
Kilmacrenan 46 C2
Kilmaine 48 D4
Kilmallock 51 E3
Kilmona 51 E4
Kilmore Quay 52 B6
Kilrea 47 F2
Kilrush 50 C2
Kilteel 52 B2
Kiltimagh 48 D3
Kiltullagh 49 E5
Kingscourt 47 F6
Kinnegad 52 A1
Kinsale 51 E5
Kinvara 48 D5
Kircubbin 47 H4
Knock 48 D3
Knockalough 50 C2
Knocktopher 52 A5

L

Lanesborough 49 F4
Larne 47 G2
Lauragh 50 B5
Laytown 47 G6
Leap 50 D6
Leighlinbridge 52 A4
Leixlip 52 B2
Letterkenny 46 D2
Lifford 46 D2
Limavady 47 E2
Limerick 51 E2
Lisbellaw 46 D4
Lisburn 47 G4
Lisdoonvarna 48 C6
Lismore 51 F4
Lisnarrick 46 D4
Lisnaskea 46 D5
Listowel 50 C3
Londonderry
  (Derry) 46 D2
Longford 49 F3
Loughrea 49 E5
Louisburgh 48 B3
Lucan 52 B2
Lukeswell 52 A5
Lurgan 47 F4

M

Macroom 50 D5
Maghera 47 F2
Magherafelt 47 F3
Malahide 52 C1
Málainn Mhóir
    (Malin More) 46 A3
Mallow 51 E4
Manorhamilton 46 C4
Markethill 47 F4
May's Corner 47 G4
Middletown 47 E4
Midleton 51 F5
Milestone 51 F2
Milford 46 D2
Millstreet 50 D4
Milltown Malbay 48 C6
Mitchelstown 51 E3
Moate 49 G5
Mohill 49 F3
Moira 47 G4
Monaghan 47 E5
Monasterevin 52 A2
Moneygall 49 F6
Moneymore 47 F3
Monivea 49 E5
Mountbellew 49 E4
Mountmellick 49 G5
Mountrath 49 G6
Mountshannon 49 E6
Moville 47 E1
Mouvalley 52 A1
Mullany's Cross 48 D2
Mullingar 49 G4
Murrisk 48 C3
Murroogh 48 C5

N

Naas 52 B2
Navan 52 B1

Nenagh 49 F6
New Ross 52 A5
Newbridge 52 B2
Newcastle *Down* 47 G5
Newcastle *S.Dub.* 52 B2
Newcastle West 50 D3
Newinn 51 F3
Newmarket 50 D4
Newmarket-on-Fergus
    50 D2
Newport *Mayo* 48 C3
Newport *N.Tipp.* 51 E2
Newry 47 F5
Newtown 51 E3
Newtown
    Mount Kennedy 52 C3
Newtownabbey 47 G3
Newtownards 47 H3
Newtownbutler 46 D5
Newtownstewart 46 D3
Ninemilehouse 51 G3
Nobber 47 F6

O

Oldcastle 47 E6
Omagh 46 D3
Oranmore 48 D5
Oughterard 48 C4

P

Pallas Green New 51 E2
Park 47 E2
Partry 48 C3
Paulstown 52 A4
Pettigo 46 C3
Pomeroy 47 E3
Pontoon 48 D2
Portadown 47 F4
Portaferry 47 H4
Portarlington 52 A2

Portavogie 47 H4
Portlaoise 49 G6
Portlaw 51 G3
Portmagee 50 A5
Portrane 52 C1
Portrush 47 F1
Portsalon 46 D1
Portstewart 47 F1
Portumna 49 F6
Poulgorm Bridge 50 C4

R

Randalstown 47 F3
Raphoe 46 D2
Rathangan 52 A2
Rathdowney 49 G6
Rathdrum 52 C3
Rathfriland 47 G5
Rathkeale 50 D3
Rathkeevin 51 F3
Rathvilly 52 B3
Ringsend 47 F2
Roscommon 49 F4
Roscrea 49 F6
Rosscarbery 50 D6
Rosslare 52 B5
Rosslare Harbour 52 C6
Rosslea 47 E5
Rostrevor 47 G5
Roundstone 48 B4
Rush 52 C1

S

Saintfield 47 G4
Schull 50 C6
Shanlaragh 50 D5
Shannon 50 D2
Shannon International
    Airport 50 D2
Shercock 47 E5

Shillelagh 52 B4
Sion Mills 46 D3
Sixmilebridge 50 D2
Sixmilecross 47 E3
Skerries 52 C1
Skibbereen 50 C6
Slane 47 F6
Sligo 46 B4
Sligo Airport 46 B4
Sneem 50 B5
South East Regional Airport
    Waterford 52 A6
Sraith Salach
    (Recess) 48 B4
Strabane 46 D3
Stradbally 52 A3
Strangford 47 H4
Stranorlar 46 D3
Strokestown 49 F3
Swinford 48 D3
Swords 52 C1

T

Taghmon 52 B5
Tallow 51 F4
Tandragee 47 F4
Tarbert 50 C2
Templemore 51 F2
Templetuohy 51 G2
Thomastown 52 A5
Thurles 51 F2
Timolin 52 B3
Tipperary 51 F3
Tobercurry 46 B5
Tower 51 E5
Tralee 50 B3
Tramore 52 A6
Trim 52 B1
Tuam 48 D4
Tulla 48 D6
Tullamore 49 G5

Tullow 52 B4
Tully 46 C4
Tulsk 49 F3

U

Urlingford 51 G2

V

Virginia 47 E6

W

Warrenpoint 47 G5
Waterford 52 A5
Watergrasshill 51 E4
Wellingtonbridge 52 B5
Westport 48 C3
Wexford 52 B5
Whitehead 47 H3
Wicklow 52 C3

Y

Youghal 51 F4

In general, distances are based on the shortest routes by classified roads.

DISTANCE IN KILOMETRES

ABERDEEN	748 282 657 509 788 719 796 370 688 613 535 903 192 904 776 246 224 735 826 694 554 165 422 505 643 597 535 860 535 401 758 603 768 1083 131 971 894 846 558 619 873 822 587 362 345 688 490
ABERYSTWYTH	513 181 260 193 347 161 366 228 228 284 469 515 307 89 682 516 171 454 162 356 770 293 269 242 309 159 342 199 417 446 253 253 486 582 374 353 276 251 118 319 406 175 525 944 159 309
AYR	457 318 588 556 595 147 488 428 372 740 129 704 577 217 58 534 663 428 391 322 222 332 480 435 334 638 335 235 594 439 568 882 156 770 694 645 378 418 672 659 394 79 504 488 332
BIRMINGHAM	177 136 156 160 310 32 67 146 309 458 252 271 626 460 83 264 238 206 714 237 172 70 135 143 182 129 319 255 81 107 431 525 319 232 181 119 70 211 234 73 472 888 42 196
BRADFORD	307 240 337 168 193 117 55 424 314 423 354 488 322 253 347 243 104 565 99 16 159 120 105 314 57 154 279 119 267 601 381 489 395 353 59 159 373 343 109 334 739 207 53
BRISTOL	234 65 441 147 203 287 313 590 119 225 758 591 55 316 329 340 845 369 318 184 266 256 190 260 467 342 218 111 298 657 185 144 76 279 163 113 254 205 603 1019 99 341
CAMBRIDGE	290 409 124 154 187 185 525 358 434 725 559 195 107 396 208 776 347 228 110 137 301 87 245 365 101 132 127 537 591 425 205 221 186 227 208 98 223 621 950 183 239
CARDIFF	447 180 233 323 361 596 171 168 763 597 90 365 314 391 851 375 354 217 307 261 239 271 501 394 248 160 345 663 238 211 140 288 167 177 303 222 609 1025 118 378
CARLISLE	341 282 225 593 148 557 460 316 150 387 516 349 244 400 75 180 333 289 188 491 188 93 448 292 420 736 213 624 547 499 225 271 526 512 240 160 573 341 185
COVENTRY	66 149 278 490 263 317 658 491 93 232 278 190 745 269 186 38 120 183 151 160 327 223 80 80 441 557 329 205 166 126 109 184 202 105 503 919 69 203
DERBY	80 329 417 317 316 597 431 148 262 247 148 669 208 111 47 82 129 202 93 258 215 25 159 496 483 384 285 237 57 103 263 253 54 443 843 108 134
DONCASTER	371 341 403 379 542 376 227 294 268 74 593 155 47 110 61 135 261 83 182 225 70 225 582 408 470 352 317 29 164 330 289 107 388 767 187 55
DOVER	714 389 523 953 749 291 204 560 400 966 551 419 292 326 465 123 442 555 264 322 214 568 781 455 205 252 376 391 227 135 387 785 1139 306 429
EDINBURGH	705 608 211 71 535 631 497 359 248 223 310 447 404 336 646 336 167 563 407 568 884 67 771 695 646 363 419 673 627 388 217 421 489 295
EXETER	334 873 707 170 403 445 457 961 484 440 299 383 371 273 376 587 454 334 227 176 772 69 200 142 374 275 170 338 320 719 1135 215 458
FISHGUARD	766 611 239 528 252 450 865 387 363 330 398 253 401 293 511 534 341 323 513 676 401 380 303 346 207 346 456 264 515 1038 238 403
FORT WILLIAM	177 704 833 618 561 105 392 502 650 605 504 808 504 410 764 609 737 1044 164 940 864 815 547 588 842 828 556 295 282 658 501
GLASGOW	537 666 462 394 270 225 336 483 439 338 642 338 246 598 453 571 883 92 774 697 649 381 422 676 662 390 135 444 491 335
GLOUCESTER	282 285 286 791 315 255 129 212 209 165 206 402 296 164 77 349 603 237 171 111 201 123 140 228 151 549 965 45 278
HARWICH	504 301 884 454 337 217 230 409 120 352 473 102 240 208 581 699 469 244 265 294 335 252 95 331 729 1057 287 347
HOLYHEAD	339 722 275 252 283 318 149 428 189 399 467 273 357 624 565 512 452 397 245 167 421 479 192 367 900 245 292
HULL	612 198 92 153 71 200 286 152 190 235 129 269 636 427 524 396 360 104 246 375 315 182 407 786 256 60
INVERNESS	482 562 700 655 594 850 594 419 814 659 827 1151 180 1030 954 905 615 678 932 879 646 399 177 747 592
KENDAL	127 273 282 130 427 124 159 444 257 359 668 308 558 493 429 189 211 466 493 179 248 658 285 144
LEEDS	154 109 115 303 67 150 268 114 262 613 376 501 389 348 54 169 368 332 115 347 735 218 39
LEICESTER	82 174 160 141 288 183 41 114 479 514 367 239 204 100 123 217 212 92 495 873 107 164
LINCOLN	188 211 136 245 164 58 196 562 471 450 321 286 71 192 302 239 137 458 829 176 114
LIVERPOOL	334 54 247 339 155 263 552 403 440 390 316 114 92 368 386 82 338 766 163 154
LONDON	310 439 179 203 92 452 665 340 114 136 256 259 123 65 255 653 1023 180 313
MANCHESTER	233 311 132 254 563 422 453 388 323 63 113 360 387 73 362 773 180 116
NEWCASTLE UPON TYNE	409 257 411 768 249 658 545 523 209 343 517 471 312 262 604 384 143
NORWICH	203 233 651 680 541 327 335 249 327 322 158 323 620 1031 301 292
NOTTINGHAM	156 512 475 399 283 246 61 133 262 236 79 463 834 123 125
OXFORD	405 637 293 125 101 208 166 104 155 185 583 999 92 274
PENZANCE	951 124 381 321 552 454 351 516 499 897 1313 393 637
PERTH	839 762 714 429 486 741 693 455 228 354 556 361
PLYMOUTH	268 209 440 342 239 405 387 785 1201 281 525
PORTSMOUTH	68 337 286 30 179 311 710 1126 208 407
SALISBURY	295 231 36 200 259 656 1077 153 372
SHEFFIELD	134 314 281 76 392 787 164 83
SHREWSBURY	252 311 59 440 850 77 207
SOUTHAMPTON	187 288 688 1103 176 384
SOUTHEND-ON-SEA	308 706 1053 244 343
STOKE-ON-TRENT	401 817 105 153
STRANRAER	582 503 346
THURSO	921 720
WORCESTER	238
YORK	

DISTANCE IN MILES

ABERDEEN	
ABERYSTWYTH	465
AYR	175 319
BIRMINGHAM	408 112 284
BRADFORD	316 161 198 110
BRISTOL	490 120 365 85 191
CAMBRIDGE	447 215 345 97 149 148
CARDIFF	494 100 370 99 209 40 180
CARLISLE	228 228 91 192 104 274 254 278
COVENTRY	428 142 303 20 120 91 77 112 212
DERBY	381 142 266 42 73 126 96 145 175 41
DONCASTER	332 176 231 91 34 179 116 200 140 93 50
DOVER	561 291 460 192 264 194 115 225 369 173 204 230
EDINBURGH	119 320 80 285 195 367 325 370 92 304 259 212 444
EXETER	561 191 437 157 263 74 223 106 346 163 197 250 242 438
FISHGUARD	502 56 358 168 220 140 270 104 286 197 196 235 325 378 207
FORT WILLIAM	153 424 135 389 303 471 451 474 196 409 371 337 592 131 543 476
GLASGOW	139 321 36 286 200 368 347 371 93 305 268 234 465 44 439 380 110
GLOUCESTER	456 106 332 51 157 34 121 56 241 58 92 141 181 333 106 148 437 334
HARWICH	514 282 412 164 216 197 67 227 321 144 163 183 127 393 250 328 518 414 175
HOLYHEAD	431 101 266 148 150 205 246 195 217 173 154 167 348 309 277 157 384 287 177 313
HULL	344 221 243 128 65 211 129 243 152 118 92 46 249 223 284 280 348 250 178 187 210
INVERNESS	103 479 200 444 351 525 482 529 248 463 416 369 600 154 597 537 66 168 492 549 449 380
KENDAL	262 182 138 147 61 229 215 233 47 167 129 96 342 139 301 240 243 140 196 282 171 123 299
LEEDS	314 167 207 107 10 197 142 220 112 116 69 29 260 193 273 226 312 209 158 209 156 57 349 79
LEICESTER	400 150 298 43 99 114 68 135 207 24 29 68 182 278 186 205 404 300 80 135 176 95 435 170 96
LINCOLN	372 192 271 84 74 166 85 191 179 74 51 38 202 251 238 247 376 273 132 143 197 44 407 175 67 51
LIVERPOOL	332 99 208 89 65 159 187 162 117 114 80 84 289 209 231 157 313 210 130 254 93 125 369 81 71 108 117
LONDON	536 213 397 113 195 118 55 148 305 94 125 162 76 402 170 249 502 399 102 75 266 178 528 265 188 100 131 208
MANCHESTER	332 124 208 80 35 162 152 169 117 99 58 51 275 209 234 182 313 210 128 219 117 95 369 77 41 88 84 33 193
NEWCASTLE UPON TYNE	249 259 146 199 96 290 227 311 58 203 160 113 345 104 365 317 255 153 250 294 248 118 260 99 93 179 152 153 273 145
NORWICH	471 277 369 159 173 213 63 245 278 139 133 140 164 350 282 332 475 371 184 63 290 146 506 276 166 114 102 211 111 193 254
NOTTINGHAM	374 157 273 50 74 140 82 154 182 50 16 44 200 253 208 212 378 281 102 150 170 80 410 160 71 26 36 96 126 82 160 126
OXFORD	477 157 353 67 166 69 79 100 261 49 99 140 133 353 141 201 458 355 48 129 222 167 514 223 163 71 123 164 57 158 255 145 97
PENZANCE	673 302 548 288 374 185 334 214 457 274 308 362 353 549 109 319 653 552 217 361 388 395 715 415 381 298 349 343 281 350 477 405 318 252
PERTH	81 362 97 326 237 408 367 412 133 346 301 254 485 42 480 420 102 57 375 434 351 265 112 191 234 320 293 251 413 262 155 423 295 396 591
PLYMOUTH	603 232 479 198 304 115 264 148 387 205 239 292 283 479 43 249 584 481 147 291 318 326 640 347 311 228 280 273 211 281 409 336 248 182 77 521
PORTSMOUTH	556 219 431 144 245 90 128 131 340 127 177 219 128 432 124 236 537 433 106 152 281 246 593 307 242 149 199 242 71 241 339 203 176 78 237 474 167
SALISBURY	526 172 401 112 219 47 138 87 310 104 147 197 156 402 88 188 507 403 69 165 247 224 562 266 216 127 178 196 85 201 325 208 153 63 200 444 130 42
SHEFFIELD	347 156 235 74 37 173 116 179 140 78 36 18 234 226 232 215 340 237 125 183 152 64 382 117 34 62 44 71 159 39 130 155 38 129 343 267 274 210 184
SHREWSBURY	384 73 260 43 99 101 142 104 169 68 64 102 243 260 171 129 365 262 76 208 104 153 421 131 105 76 119 57 161 70 213 203 83 103 282 302 213 178 143 83
SOUTHAMPTON	542 198 418 131 232 70 129 110 327 114 163 205 141 418 106 215 523 420 87 157 261 233 580 290 229 135 187 229 76 224 321 200 163 65 218 460 148 19 23 195 156
SOUTHEND-ON-SEA	511 252 409 145 213 158 61 188 318 126 157 180 84 389 210 289 515 411 142 59 298 196 546 306 206 132 148 239 40 241 293 98 147 96 321 431 252 111 124 180 193 116
STOKE-ON-TRENT	365 109 245 46 68 127 139 138 149 65 34 66 240 241 199 164 346 242 94 206 119 113 402 111 72 57 85 51 158 45 194 201 49 115 310 283 241 193 161 47 37 179 191
STRANRAER	225 326 49 293 207 375 386 378 99 313 275 241 488 135 447 320 183 84 341 453 228 253 248 154 216 308 285 210 406 225 163 385 288 362 557 141 488 441 408 244 273 427 439 249
THURSO	210 587 313 552 460 633 590 637 356 571 524 477 708 262 705 645 175 276 600 657 559 488 110 409 457 524 515 476 636 480 376 641 518 621 816 220 746 700 670 489 528 686 654 508 362
WORCESTER	428 99 303 26 128 62 114 73 212 43 67 116 190 304 133 148 409 305 28 178 152 159 464 177 136 67 109 102 112 112 239 187 76 57 244 345 175 129 95 102 48 109 152 65 312 572
YORK	304 192 206 122 33 212 149 235 115 126 83 34 267 183 285 250 311 208 173 216 181 38 368 89 24 102 71 96 194 72 89 182 78 173 396 224 326 253 231 52 129 239 213 95 215 447 148